The Bull Terrier

– A Complete Anthology of the Dog –

1850-1940

ISBN No.
978-14455-2809-0 (Paperback)
978-14455-2700-0 (Hardback)

British Library Cataloguing-in-Publication Data
A catalogue record for this book is available from
the British Library

VDB

www.vintagedogbooks.com

Contents

Containing chapters from the following sources:

Breeding, Training, Management, Diseases, Etc, Of Dogs; Together With An Easy And Agreeable Method Of Instructing All Breeds Of Dogs In A Great Variety Of Amusing And Useful Performances, Including 31 Illustrations Of The Different Breeds Of Dogs. **Francis Butler.** 1857..*page 1*

House Dogs And Sporting Dogs - Their Varieties, Points, Management, Training, Breeding, Rearing And Diseases. **John Meyrick.** 1861..*page 2*

The Dogs Of The British Islands. Being A Series Articles Of The Points Of Their Various Breeds, And The Treatment Of The Diseases To Which They Are Subject. **J. H. Walsh.** 1867..*page 4*

Terrier Dogs: Showing The Best Methods Of Breeding, Rearing, Feeding, Cropping, Physicing, Cure Of Diseases, Etc., With A Description Of The Points And Properties Of The Principal Breeds Of Dogs. **Ed James.** 1873.........*page 10*

The Illustrated Book Of The Dog. **Vero Shaw.** 1879.
....*page 14*

A History And Description Of The Modern Dogs Of Great Britain And Ireland. (Terriers). **Rawdon B. Lee.** 1894...*page 23*

My Dog And I - Being A Concise Treatise Of The Various Breeds Of Dogs Their Origins And Uses. Written Expressly For The Novice. **H. W. Huntington.** 1897.
....*page 54*

The Show Dog - Being A Book Devoted To Describing The Cardinal Virtues And Objectionable Features Of All The Breeds Of Dogs From The Show Ring Standpoint, With Mode Of Treatment Of The Dog Both In Health And Sickness. **H. W. Huntington.** 1901.......................*page 56*

Dog Shows And Doggy People. **C. H. Lane.** 1902....*page 59*

British Dogs - Their Points, Selection, And Show
Preparation - With Illustrations Of Typical Dogs.
W. D. Drury. 1903...*page 60*

The Twentieth Century Dog (Non Sporting) - Compiled
From The Contributions Of Over Five Hundred Experts.
Vol. I. **Herbert Compton.** 1904............................*page 69*

The Dog Book - A Popular History Of The Dog, With
Practical Care And Management Of House, Kennel, And
Exhibition Dogs - Volume II.
James Watson. 1906...*page 79*

The Kennel Encyclopaedia - Vol. I. A B D To C O L.
J. Sidney Turner. 1907.......................................*page 89*

The New Book Of The Dog - A Comprehensive Natural
History Of British Dogs And Their Foreign Relatives, With
Chapters On Law, Breeding, Kennel Management, And
Veterinary Treatment. Vol. III. **Robert Leighton.**
1907...*page 107*

British Terriers: Their Breeding, Management And
Training For Show Or Work. **J. Maxtee.** 1909.........*page 114*

Dogs And All About Them. **Robert Leighton.** 1910.
....*page 115*

The Sporting Bull Terrier - A Book Of General Information
Valuable To Owners, Trainers, Handlers, And Breeders Of
Bull Terriers. **Eugene Glass.** 1915......................*page 120*

Terriers. **Darley Matheson.** 1922........................*page 141*

Dogs And How To Know Them - With Notes As To Their
Care And Management And Other Information. Including
A Standard Of Excellence And A Complete List Of Books
On Dogs From 1800 In The British Museum.
Edward C. Ash. 1925......................................*page 144*

The Practical Dog Book - With Chapters On The Authentic History Of All Varieties Hitherto Unpublished, And A Veterinary Guide And Dosage Section, And Information On Advertising And On Exporting To All Parts Of The World. **Edward C. Ash.** 1930..............................*page 146*

About Our Dogs - The Breeds And Their Management. **A. Croxton Smith.** 1931.....................................*page 152*

Dogs Of The World - The Author And Dogs - History And Origins Of Man's Best Friend - Care And General Management - Feeding - Rearing - Exhibiting - Common Diseases, Etc. **Arthur Craven.** 1931......................*page 158*

Hutchinson's Dog Encyclopaedia - An Invaluable Work Of International Importance (Alphabetically Arranged For Easy Reference) On Breeds Of Dogs Of Every Country, With Full Veterinary Advice In Cases Of Accidents Or Ailments, Etc., On Their Care And Home Treatment, Contributed By The Most Eminent Authorities. Volume I - A To Fo. **Walter Hutchinson.** 1935......................*page 160*

The Book Of Dogs. **Stanley West.** 1935.................*page 183*

Bull Terriers. **V. C. Hollender.**............................*page 191*

Apt as a scholar, faithful as a friend
Well armed and ready, valiant to defend

BULL TERRIER.

THE BULL-TERRIER.

It is a current axiom among dog fanciers that no gameness can be got in any dog, without a taint, or cross, of the Bulldog. The Bull-terrier is a signal proof of this theory; for the pure Terrier, though active, is by no means distinguished for pluck; whereas the Bull-terrier is scarcely inferior in this quality to the Bulldog himself, and in vivacity and activity he surpasses him.

The Bull-terrier varies greatly, according to the predominance of either the Terrier or the Bulldog blood. It is difficult, however, to decide from the appearance of the dog, how much he owes to each breed. As a rule, when the nose is short, and the jaw much underhung, the bulldog predominates; but this is not invariable, for it is no unusual to see both long and short faced puppies in the same litter of Bull-terriers.

There are certain marks by which the Bull-terrier may always be distinguished: namely, a great breadth of *jowl*, which gives enormous power to the grip; depth in the *brisket* and *chest*; a peculiar roundness of the *stifle-joint*, which is slightly turned out, accompanied by a well-let-down *hock*; but the most characteristic and unmistakeable point is the small *eye*, which becomes round the moment that the dog's attention is excited; the pure terrier's. eye always remains long and narrow. A Bull-terrier, in addition to these points, should have straight *legs*, and strong, well developed *hind quarters*.

His *shoulders* should be particularly well covered with muscle; his *neck* should be lean and hard; his *loins* strong; and his *tail* fine, and not carried high. His *height* varies from 10 to 20 inches, and he weighs from 10 to 30 lbs. or even more. The best *colours* are pure white, and pure red, or white with patches of brindle. Black and tan, white and tan, and brindle, are often seen.

For every quality which makes the dog a valued companion to man, the Bull-terrier is unsurpassed by any other breed. He will hunt for him, watch his house, and fight for him; he is teachable and intelligent; he is the best-tempered companion and the most faithful friend.

THE BULL TERRIER.

The Bull Terrier, like his chief progenitor, the bulldog, is now without a vocation, dog fights being prohibited by law, and rat pits being equally out of the question.   But, unlike the bulldog, he is an excellent companion for the male sex, being a little too violent in his quarrels to make him desirable as a ladies' pet. Careful crossing—said to be with the terrier, but also alleged to be with the greyhound or foxhound, or both—has produced a handsome, symmetrical animal, without a vestige of the repugnant and brutal expression of the bulldog, and with the elegant lines of the greyhound, though considerably thickened in their proportions. From fifteen to twenty years' ago, Mr. Hinks, of Birmingham, held undisputed sway in this breed with a kennel of white dogs, in which a "Madman" always existed; but the identical animal varied almost every year, as he was enticed away y the high bids of the lovers of this breed.   At that time there was still a slight reminder of the bull in the comparatively full lip; but in 1868 Old Victor suddenly appeared from the Black Country without this appendage, and with such a fine form of head and frame that he succeeded in gaining the flats of the judges

4

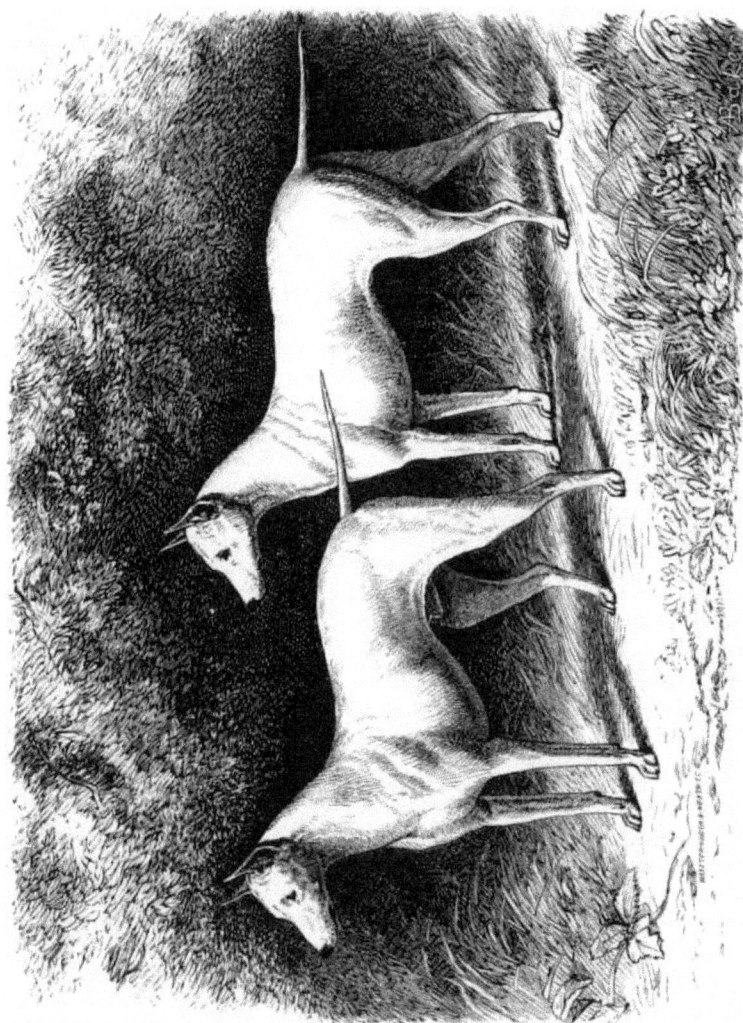

Mr. Vero Shaw's White English Terriers "Silvio" and "Sylph."

5

in his favour; and his type has since then been installed as that which is to be considered the proper one for the breed. Nothing is known of his pedigree, and all the guesses made at his greyhound parentage are purely hypothetical. He was, like all the "Madmen" of Mr. Hinks's breeding, a pure white; but when put to an equally all-white bitch, one of the produce was the celebrated "mark-eyed" dog Young Victor, who won nearly every prize open to him till his career was cut short by poison at the Hull Show of 1875. His son Tarquin whose portrait is appended to this article, is, however, a worthy representative of the breed.

The bull terrier is still judged by the fighting standard—that is to say, he must have all the points, mental as well as bodily, which are necessary to the fighting dog. If of pure bull parentage or nearly so, he is unfitted for the office; for, instead of laying hold and shaking his adversary for a time with great force, and then changing to a fresh place of attack, as the fighting dog should do, he keeps his hold tenaciously, and never changes it but on compulsion. The infusion of terrier, greyhound, or foxhound, or whatever may be the cross, gives activity of body in addition to the above mental peculiarity, and thus is created an animal calculated to take his own part in any combat, whether with one of his own kind or with any of our native larger vermin, or even with the smaller *felidæ* of other lands. His temper is sufficiently under control to prevent his intentionally injuring his master, under the severest provocation, and he is admitted to be, of all dogs, the most efficient protector against attack in proportion to his size and muscular powers. He is a very cleanly animal in the house, and many years ago I had one which, being by accident confined in my bedroom surreptitiously for four days, under the care of a person who fed him, but neglected to let him out as directed, for fear of discovery, never once relieved himself of any of his secretions, by which he very nearly lost his life. Show dogs of this breed accustomed to the house, if left on their benches, are peculiarly liable to injury from this cause, which is indeed a fertile source of mischief to all dogs, and the higher their courage the worse for their health. The bull terrier is a capital vermin dog, and, if small enough, "goes to ground" well at fox or badger; but is too severe in his attack, his tendency being to kill rather than bolt his fox. For this reason the slightest visible cross of .bull with the fox terrier is objected to; but for all vermin work above ground the bull terrier of the present day is admirably suited.

Nothing reliable is known of the pedigrees of any of the best specimens of the bull terrier in these days; and in former years, while the dog pits of Birmingham, Walsall, Stafford, Westminster, &c., still existed, the best strains were equally without recognised paternity beyond the first generation, breeders selecting a well-known fighting dog to mate with an equally famous bitch, whose prowess had been proved on more than one occasion. It is true that certain strains were famous among the "fancy;" but they seldom existed long, subsequent victories bringing out fresh favourites, and these being again displaced by the fortune of war, as fickle in the pit as elsewhere. At present breeders go back to Old Victor as the origin of all the best dogs, and improving upon Mr. Hinks's strain—which

6

had probably been too much in-bred—in size, symmetry, and notably in face and lip. The points are as follows :—

POINTS OF THE BULL TERRIER.

Skull	Value.	Shoulder and chest	Value.	Coat	Value.
Skull	15	Shoulder and chest ...	15	Coat	5
Face and teeth	10	Back	10	Colour	5
Ears	5	Legs	10	Tail	5
Neck	5	Feet	5	Symmetry	10
	35		40		25

Grand Total 100.

1. The *skull* (value 15) should be long and flat, wedge-shaped, *i.e.*, wide behind with the smaller end at the place of the brow, which should not be at all prominent. The line from the occiput to the end of the nose should be as straight as possible, without either brow or hollow in front of the eyes. This line is never absolutely straight, but the nearer it approaches to a straight line the better. The skull should, however, be "broken up," but not to anything like the same extent as in the bulldog.

2. *Face, eyes, lips, and teeth* (value 10).—The jaws must be long and powerful, nose large and black (though many otherwise first-rate dogs have had spotted or "butterfly" noses, notably Mr. Godfree's Old Puss). *Eyes* small, black, and sparkling. The upper *lip* should be as tight over the jaw as possible, any superfluous skin or approach to chop being undesirable. The under *lip* also should be small. The *teeth* should be regular in shape, meeting exactly, without any deviation from the straight line. A pig jaw is as great a fault as being underhung.

3. The *ears* (value 5) are always cropped for show purposes, and the degree of perfection with which this has been accomplished is generally taken into consideration. They should be brought to a fine point and exactly match. In their uncropped state they vary a good deal in shape, and seldom reach their full proportion till after teething.

4. The *neck* (value 5) should be rather long, and gracefully set into the shoulders, from which it should taper to the head, without any throatiness or approach to dewlap, as in the bulldog.

5. *Shoulders and chest* (value 15).—The shoulders should be strong and slanting with a wide and deep chest; but the last ribs are not very deep, though brought well back towards the hips.

6. The *back* (value 10) should be short and well furnished with muscle, running forward between the shoulder blades in a firm bundle on each side.

7. The *legs* (value 10).—The forelegs should be long and perfectly straight, the elbows lying in the same plane as the shoulder points, and not outside them, as in the bulldog. The hind legs should also be long and muscular, with straight hocks placed low down, *i.e.*, near the ground.

7

MR. VERO SHAW'S BULL TERRIERS "TARQUIN" AND "NAPPER."

8. The *feet* (value 5) are rather long than cat-like; but the toes should be well arched and close together.

9. The *coat* (value 5) must be short and close, but hard rather than silky, though when in show condition it should shine from constant friction.

10. The *colour* (value 5) for show purposes must be pure white, though there are many well-shaped dogs of other colours. This is, however, purely a fancy breed, and as such there is not the slightest reason why an arbitrary rule should not be made, as it was without doubt in this case, and it is useless to show a dog of any other colour.

11. The *tail* (value 5) or stern should be set on low, fine in bone, and carried straight out without any curl over the back.

12. Of *symmetry* (value 10) this dog shows a considerable amount, all his points being agreeable to the eye of the artist. Any deviation from a due proportion should therefore be punished accordingly.

The dogs I have selected for illustration are, first, Mr. Vero Shaw's celebrated Tarquin, to represent the class above 20lb., he being 44lb. in weight, and having won at Birmingham, Darlington, Wolverhampton, Northampton, Maidstone, Cork, Alexandra Palace, Crystal Palace, and other shows. Tarquin is by Young Victor out of a bitch called Puss, and was bred by Mr. C. L. Boyce, of Birmingham. Secondly, for the small class under 20lb., I have chosen Napper, belonging to the same gentleman. He weighs 18lb., and is by Bardle's Napper (a son of Mr. Shirley's celebrated Nelson, who was admitted to be the best dog of his day) out of Minnie. He has been successful at the Crystal Palace, Cork, and other shows.

Since the third edition of the "Dogs of the British Islands" appeared, one of the great Birmingham breeders has ceased to exist for show purposes; for Mr. J. F. Godfree has disposed of his entire kennel of bull terriers to Mr. Vero Shaw, who almost monopolised the prizes in this class for some time, and then, in his turn, gave them up, together with the whole of his kennel. The name of Mr. Hinks of Birmingham, too, has recently disappeared from the list of exhibitors, most of his stud having passed into the hands of Mr. Hartley, of Altrincham, who afterwards disposed of the best to Mr. G. A. Dawes, of Leamington. Messrs. Battersby, of Bolton; Chorley, of Kendal; Tredennick; Parkin, of Sheffield; and Miller, of Walsall, frequently show first-rate specimens of this breed, which appears to have recently taken a new lease in public favour; for its unusual docility, if properly managed, and its intelligence, enable a bull terrier to learn almost anything that a dog can be taught; whilst its pluck is indisputable, and its mute system of attack renders it on many occasions superior to a fox terrier, who, when working, is apt to give tongue too loudly.

Reynolds.

THE BULL TERRIER.

The Bull Terrier is bred from the Bull Dog and English Terrier Hound, the last named being used for bringing out the fox when he is secreted in his hole and the Fox Hounds cannot get at him, and is noted for extraordinary speed, scent, and gameness, in short, he will face anything.

The first cross of Bull Terrier is generally too much like the Bull Dog, but the second shows in perfection all the attributes required for the purpose the Bull Terrier is used.

The best breed of Bull Terriers are those that come from the North of England, Yorkshire and Staffordshire. They are used for fighting, rat killing, coon, badger, and bear baiting, and make perhaps the best watch dogs. The Bull Terrier is becoming a more domestic and tractable successor to the Bull Dog uniting, as he does, the most desirable qualities and presenting a far more inviting appearance.

Whatever objections may be raised to some of the uses

terriers are employed in, dogs will be dogs and "delight to bark and bite," as Watts the psalmist has to truthfully sung.

No one however has such a passionate love for that detestable "varmint" the rat, as to object to the destruction of the same. It is as natural for a good dog to kill rats as for a cat to kill mice.

POINTS AND PROPERTIES OF A PERFECT BULL TERRIER.

His head should be long, the muzzle sharp, the jaw level—not underhung, which is a disfigurement and also prevents a dog punishing his adversary. The under jaw should display great power, and the neck should be long.

The chest is wide, the shoulders sloping and powerful, the loins and back strong, the hind quarters and thighs muscular. The tail should be fine and sting-like but not bare, carried gaily but not "hooped."

The fore legs should be straight with a slight angle at the pastern. The bone of the leg must be as large as possible and the muscle of the fore arm as well as the tendons of the pasterns and toes, proportionably strong. If the foot is not perfectly straight, it must turn in, not out. In shape it should be round and cat-like, but very highly arched toes are apt to give way. Sole hard and thick. The hind quarters must be as strong as possible, wide as well as deep. Bone of pastern strong and large; hocks strong and straight.

The coat throughout is fine and short, and it should lie smoothly as in a well dressed racehorse. Pure white, with a black eye and nose, is the most approved color, but white with colored ears or a patch on the eyes is highly appreciated. As in the Bull Dog the color should be "whole" and, when spotted, correspond with the colors of the Bull Dog.

His weight varies from twelve up to thirty-five pounds or more.

His appearance resembles that of the terrier, except that he is wider across the skull and possesses more strength and stamina.

11

BULL TERRIER.

THE BULL TERRIER, "WATERFORD JACK."

No breed of dog is at present making such a rapid advance in public favour as the modern and improved Bull-terrier, and its well-deserved popularity seems far more likely to be permanent than that of other breeds which have in turn been taken up only to be dismissed by their owners when their lack of intelligence, cowardice, or general inutility, has proved them to be unworthy of the patronage bestowed upon them. The breed as it now exists is comparatively of recent manufacture, and is indisputably the result of judicious selection from and with the well-known Bull *and* Terrier of the Midland counties. This dog, in its turn, was brought into existence by crossing the Bull-dog with the white English Terrier, and was produced in the first instance by the supporters and lovers of dog-fighting, who wished to obtain a longer and more punishing head than that possessed by a pure Bull-dog. This latter cross, in the first instance, produced a sullen-looking, thick-skulled dog, showing slight indications of symmetry in his composition, but still admirably adapted for the purpose for which he was called into existence. How the present show Bull-terrier arose from such a dog is more or less the subject of conjecture, for no trustworthy particulars of its origin are obtainable from the part of the country where it first appeared; but there is little cause to differ from the general impression, that many of the larger-sized show specimens have Greyhound blood in their veins, whilst the smaller breed is more closely allied with the English Terrier than is desirable.

We ourselves have been applied to by a gentleman whose name is well known in the coursing world, for permission to cross some of his Greyhound bitches with the Bull-terriers Tarquin and Sallust. The object of this was his desire to instil stamina and pluck into his breed, which he fancied was degenerating in these qualifications, and need not be gone into here, though it will, with his permission, be noticed in the chapter on Greyhounds. The result of the first Bull-terrier cross, in each instance, was a large-framed, though light-boned and rather narrow-chested dog, with, for a Bull-terrier, very snipy jaws, and possessing the peculiar *action* of the Greyhound in a marked degree. The difficulty of breeding out the last point alluded to struck us the moment we saw the animals move; and the original introducers of this blood into the Bull-terrier—if there are such persons in existence—deserve considerable credit for their perseverance in their endeavours. However, not having the slightest desire to experimentalise in the matter, we are unable to give further information as regards the cross, so far as it affects the Bull-terrier, beyond the fact that the dog puppies were at once destroyed by their owner, the females alone being retained by him for the purpose of working out his experiment.

One of the earliest records we can find of the Bull-terrier is in one of the editions of Blaine's "Rural Sports," in which allusion is made to the breed in the following words:—
" A large breed of English Terriers has of late sprung up, most of which are rough-coated, but a few others are smooth. These, by being crossed with the Bull-dog, have gained undaunted courage in attacking the higher order of vermin—as the badger, &c."

In the "Naturalists' Library," too, by Sir William Jardine, published in 1843, the breed

14

is thus alluded to :—" In England the cross of Terriers is perceptible in sheep and cattle dogs, but most of all in the breed called Bull-terriers, because it is formed of these two varieties, and constitutes the most determined and savage race known."

From all recognised accounts the ancestors of the modern Bull-terrier must have been a rough-and-ready race, and the illustration overleaf is useful in conveying an idea to our readers of what the creatures were like. In the dog situated in the lower portion of the plate may be found the type of a really half-bred dog, showing perhaps rather more bull, especially about the flews, than was permitted in even those days of careless breeding, but still displaying some Terrier characteristics. The two dogs on the top of the steps very much resemble the Bull and Terrier still used for fighting purposes in the Midland Counties, but in form and colour they are as unlike a modern show Bull-terrier as it is possible to imagine.

To the late Mr. James Hinks, of Worcester Street, Birmingham, is due the credit of bringing the breed before the notice of the public in its later and more desirable form, and with his well-known Old Madman and Puss he farmed our leading shows for a long period. After a time, Mr. J. F. Godfree, of Birmingham, appeared in the field. His celebrated Young Victor fairly monopolised the prizes at the great exhibitions for many a day ; and on his death his mantle fell upon his son Tarquin, for some considerable time our own property, whose portrait will appear in due course amongst the coloured plates. Almost all the leading breeders of the day have dipped deeply into Hinks' Old Victor strain, whilst that of Mr. Godfree is equally well patronised ; and it is an undoubted fact that the breeding of Bull-terriers is now a much easier task than it was some time back, as the offspring of dogs belonging to the above strains are more similar in type and uniform in general appearance than is the case with those whose ancestors are of less fashionable blood.

The Bull-terrier varies in size from five pounds weight up to fifty, and thus admirers of the breed have the opportunity of selecting a dog whose size is adapted for the work or kennel accommodation at hand, which is no small recommendation in the case of those whose out-door space is limited. Though his extreme docility and intelligence render this breed of dog eminently qualified for an in-door pet, few varieties require more genuine hard work and out-door exercise to get them into show condition, as the muscles which should be so plainly visible on the fore and hind quarters of a dog in perfect trim become relaxed and flabby if his proper amount of exercise is curtailed. Many exhibitors residing in towns, and who are unable to spare sufficient time to run their dogs in the country, have adopted the expedient of making them chase a ball about their gardens for an hour or two a day, or else by hanging a piece of cat-skin on a wall, or at the end of a stick, and keeping it out of the dog's reach they cause their Terrier to exercise himself in his unceasing endeavours to obtain possession of the treasure by jumping up at it. These methods of exercising a dog in a small space may perhaps be novel to readers who are unacquainted with the devices to which many successful breeders and exhibitors are compelled to resort, in their endeavours to compete with others whose opportunities for bringing their dogs fit and well to the post are more extensive.

A very silly prejudice exists against the Bull-terrier on account of his alleged in-variable ferocity of temper and irresistible inclination to fight with all other dogs that come within his reach ; thus many would-be supporters of the breed have held aloof from it in consequence of the reports they have heard concerning him. That there is a slight founda-tion for these detractions we cannot deny, but after a pretty considerable experience of Bull-terriers we unhesitatingly affirm that the prejudice against his temper is grossly exaggerated ;

15

no breed of dog, if properly brought up and kindly treated, is more susceptible of affection towards his master, and docility and intelligence are properties which are highly developed in a Bull-terrier. Naturally a dog which may be said to be a born gladiator possesses a greater amount of courage and tenacity in his attack than animals of a gentler temperament, and a firm temper is often required to keep them in thorough discipline; but as a gentleman's companion in town or country, the Bull-terrier is unapproached by any other breed of dog. He is handsome to look at, affectionate, clean in the house, and very tricky; an excellent water dog, and, though it may be discredited by some people, we are convinced that his nose is equal to that of many dogs used in the field, though his impetuous disposition would render it a difficult matter to keep him under the severe control so essential in a field dog. As a retriever he is naturally hard-mouthed, but no breed can more easily be taught to fetch and carry on land and water, and this is, doubtless a source of amusement to many owners. It is, however, for his indomitable courage (unsurpassed even by the Bull-dog) that the Bull-terrier is so highly prized by many—for, though usually mute like the Bull-dog, his system of attack is different from that of the latter, inasmuch as, instead of hanging on to his antagonist, the Bull-terrier tears him all over; and his pluck is so great that he is able to endure an enormous amount of punishment, whilst in his turn he is mangling his foe with his powerful jaws. During more recent years, and since the retirement from the show arena of Mr. S. E. Shirley, M.P., Mr. R. J. Lloyd-Price, Mr. Godfree, and the late Mr. Hinks, the majority of the Bull-terrier prizes have come down south through the kennels of Mr. Loveys of London, Mr. Pfeil of Sutton, Mr. Alfred George of Kensal New Town (whose capital little dog Spring is well worthy of the honours he has won), Mr. Tredennick of St. Austell, Cornwall (whose grand little Bertie will long be remembered as being both good and game), and ourselves; whilst the Midland prestige has been fairly maintained by Messrs. Roocroft of Bolton, Miller of Walsall, and R. J. Hartley of Altrincham. The latter gentleman, who is a most enthusiastic lover and supporter of the breed, owns two magnificent specimens in Magnet and Violet. Authorities differ on the merits of these two famous bitches, but we most unhesitatingly give our allegiance to the former, whose sole fault is being a little light in bone. The condition, too, in which Mr. Hartley's dogs are exhibited is a model for the imitation of all Bull-terrier breeders.

Before passing on to a detailed description of the points of a Bull-terrier, a few lines should be devoted to the subject of colour. It must appear an arbitrary rule to decide that a dog of this breed should, if of any use as a show dog, be pure white; but a moment's reflection must show that there is a motive for this decision. The difficulty of eradicating the undesirable traces of Bull in his face, body, and limbs, is tremendous; and it is solely by practically adopting the theory of the survival of the fittest that a satisfactory result can be obtained. Why only white dogs were selected in the first instance we could never discover; but of this we are convinced by experience, namely, that the introduction of a heavily-marked dog into a strain of Bull-terriers has a decided tendency to cause a throw back to Bull characteristics, and this can only be attributed to the fact that the colours other than white have been less carefully bred than the more fashionable colour. We are quite prepared to admit that there are many excellent dogs of a colour other than white, but we maintain that these, though in themselves good specimens, are undesirable for breeding purposes, and should be avoided, though many of them are the offspring of highly-bred pure white dogs, themselves successful competitors at our best shows. It is a painful fact that in most litters there even now appear one or more "marked" puppies; but the danger in permitting these to be used to

ORIGINAL BULL AND TERRIER CROSS.

any extent for breeding purposes would be that very soon countless good-looking marked dogs would be shown all over the country. These being used for stud purposes would, from their markings most likely beget a still larger proportion of marked stock, and contaminate the breed we have now brought to something like the desired perfection. In short, before a breed of brindled or coloured Bull-terriers can be fairly established, several years will have to be devoted by their admirers to them, in order that they may stand on an equal footing with their white brethren as regards uniformity of shape and reliability in breeding. Young Victor, late the property of Mr. Godfree, proves the truth of this theory; though disfigured by a patch on his eye, no dog could have been more successful on the bench, and few had better opportunities of distinguishing themselves at the stud. That he could beget good stock is indisputable; but the result of his triumphs was the introduction of a class for Bull-terriers " other than white" at a Crystal Palace show, and the subsequent appearance at other exhibitions of a number of thick, heavy-headed wretches, whose introduction into a good strain of the breed would jeopardise its prospects for many a day.

No breed of dog owes more to condition on the show-bench than does the Bull-terrier. A dog of this variety exhibited in bad order has little chance of beating an inferior specimen, even under a first-class judge; and where the awards are in the hands of inexperienced judges, his chances of success would be absolutely *nil*. The fact of the intensely brilliant white so often seen in the coats of dogs at the different shows being frequently the result of art, in the application of powdered chalk, is indisputable. However, detection and subsequent disqualification often follow in the wake of such practices, and should do so, especially as—unless the dog is suffering from some irritation of the skin—a resort to powder is quite unnecessary. In cases where the skin is inflamed by heat of the blood, the application of powdered chalk may be excusable; but adopters of this method of concealment should be particularly careful to brush it thoroughly out of the coat before the dog is led into the judging-ring, or they may find their specimen disqualified. Personally, we cannot too strongly advocate the showing of dogs honestly and fairly. Prizes won by means of foul play must, in the long run, cause more feelings of remorse in the mind of the exhibitor than they do those of triumph in the moment of victory; and we have proved by personal experience that a dog in good condition, and properly washed, can win unfaked if he is good enough. Our own system of washing show Bull-terriers is very simple, though it takes time. The dog is placed standing up in a large shallow tub half filled with warm water, and is in the first instance thoroughly wetted by the water being poured over him with a bowl or saucer. Next comes the application of the soap—the sort we invariably use is the common blue and *white* (not *yellow*) mottled—and the part first operated on is the head. When this is thoroughly soaped and rinsed, the body and legs are treated in like manner, and finally the first stage of his ablutions is completed with the aid of several *clean* towels. The second part of the operation consists in rubbing him perfectly dry with bare hands, by smoothing the hair down over and over again, in the right direction, until there is no more moisture left on it. The dog is then put on a clean straw bed, and if looked after to see that he does not get out of his kennel will in the course of a couple of hours be as white as snow, and his jacket will shine like silver. The greatest care must be taken in putting on the collar after the washing is completed, as collars often get soiled inside, and if so, will inevitably blacken the dog's neck.

Preparatory to the above, however, it is always most desirable to remove the superfluous hairs from a dog's ears and muzzle before he is shown, as this operation tends to smarten him up considerably. The *inside* only of the ears are operated on, and the hairs are removed by either careful clipping or shaving. This operation however requires the assistance of both art and experience, and therefore no tyro should attempt it without the assistance of some one who is an authority on the subject. The grotesque appearance of Old Puss in the champion class at the Agricultural Hall show of 1877 should be a warning to youthful owners against turning their 'prentice hands to such delicate operations. In her case the poor wretch had the hair shaved off the *back* of her ears ; and her comical appearance caused roars of laughter amongst the breeders present. The removal of the long "smellers" from the muzzle, however, is an easy matter if the dog is not inclined to bite. If he is, it is generally a good plan to get a friend to perform the operation, care being taken, however, only to remove the smellers and *long* eyebrows, nothing more. Having given the above hints upon getting up Bull-terriers for show purposes, we have nothing further to add before passing on to a description of this breed, beyond again impressing on our readers the great importance of *muscular development* in this breed. They must recollect they are showing the gladiator of the canine race, and a fighting dog should, in our opinion, be exhibited thoroughly trained ; that is, muscular and light in flesh. Hard work and good wholesome food will alone put on muscle and take off fat ; and the more a Bull-terrier gets of either the happier he is.

It frequently happens in showing Bull-terriers that medicine has to be given to reduce the weight in the small sizes a pound or two, in order to qualify them for a certain class. The best physic to use under such circumstances is either ordinary black-draught, or buckthorn and castor-oil. As a rule we always postponed physicking until the week before the show, hoping that exercise would reduce the dog, and medicine could be avoided. Again, if a dog is weakened by aperients too long before a show there is a great chance of his losing muscle, which would be greatly against him on the bench. If you have a dog very near the required weight, feed him lightly the night before the show, and give him one drink of water. The last thing let him have a good dose of buckthorn and oil, and don't feed him or give him a drink until he is judged, when he will probably have lost half a pound weight, if previously in good condition.

It would now be as well to go through the points of this variety, and we will begin as usual with

The Head, which should be flat, wide between the ears, and wedge-shaped ; that is, tapering from the sides of the head to the nose ; no stop or indentation between the eyes is permissible, and the cheek-bones should not be visible.

The Teeth should be powerful and perfectly regular— an undershot or overhung mouth being very objectionable—and the lips thin and tight ; that is, only just sufficient to cover the teeth, and not pendulous, as in the case of the Bull-dog.

The Nose, large, quite black, and damp, with the nostrils well developed.

The Eyes must be small, and very black. As regards shape, the oblong is preferable to the round eye.

The Ears are almost invariably cropped, and should stand perfectly upright. This cutting of the ears is now almost reduced to a science, and no inexperienced persons should attempt it, as if improperly manipulated, what is intended as both an ornament and a convenience to the dog becomes an unsightly disfigurement.

The Neck should be moderately long and arched, free from all traces of dewlap, and strongly set upon the shoulders.

The Shoulders, slanting and very muscular, set firmly on the chest, which should be wide.

The Fore legs should be moderately high and *perfectly straight*, and the dog must stand

19

well *on* them, for they do not, as in the case of the Bull-dog, turn outwards at the shoulders.

Feet, moderately long and compact, with the toes well arched.

Body, deep at chest, and well ribbed up.

Hind legs, long and very muscular, with hocks straight, and near the ground.

Coat, short, and rather harsh to the touch.

Colour, white.

Tail or *Stern* fine, set on low, and not carried up, but as straight out from the back as possible.

In general appearance the Bull-terrier is a symmetrical-looking dog, apparently gifted with great strength and activity, and of a lively and determined disposition.

In spite of the popularity of the breed, it is a lamentable fact that its progress towards

NELSON, SMALL-SIZED BULL-TERRIER, LATE THE PROPERTY OF MR. S. E. SHIRLEY, M.P.

perfection is at present very slow. It has not had fair-play at the hands of show committees, and with its kinsmen—the Black-and-tan and White English Terriers—usually has to put up with a judge who is engaged for other classes and takes these as an addition to his other labours. Thus we see, show after show, dogs gaining prizes in these classes which do not show one atom of *Terrier* character in their composition, being great, lumbering, heavy-lipped, phlegmatical, cow-faced wretches, with no vivacity or "go" in them. These are just the dogs to be avoided by a Terrier breeder, and their success is highly prejudicial to the breeds. Naturally the breed suffers, and unless some one with private influence gets justice done to it, the Bull-terrier will drift back to the mongrel state it emerged from when it was first fortunate enough to receive the patronage of powerful friends. As a proof of the unsatisfactory state the breed is in at present, we have been unable to find a small dog possessing sufficient merit to entitle it to a place in our list of illustrations, and we are therefore thrown back upon a portrait of Nelson, late the property of Mr. S. E. Shirley, M.P. This dog was a really first-rate specimen of the small-sized Bull-terrier, and showed merit enough to deserve a place in any work on the dog; and it is the more to be regretted that, in spite of the increase of breeders, the quality of the breed, especially the small ones, has not improved in proportion, as it unquestionably should have done.

A real Bull-terrier of 16 pounds weight will do all a Fox-terrier of 20 pounds weight can do, and then, if necessary, kill the Fox-terrier ninety times out of a hundred. Yet the Fox-terrier exhibitors have it nearly all their own way in electing judges, and getting special prizes awarded them, merely because, being a more numerous variety, they have more powerful friends at Court, and are not required to show the courage and resolution, lacking which, a Bull-terrier would be absolutely worthless.

Tarquin, the subject of our illustration, was bred by Mr. Charles Louis Boyce of Birmingham, in 1873, and was purchased from him by us in 1876. He is a pure white dog, weighing about 45 pounds, and is by Young Victor out of Puss, by Gambler out of Young Puss ; Young Victor, by Old Victor out of Steel's Puss ; Gambler, by Turk out of Kit, dam of Old Madman ; Turk, by Rebel out of Fly. Tarquin has taken the following prizes : First Wolverhampton, first Northampton, first Birmingham, 1874 ; champion Nottingham, first Birmingham, first Alexandra Palace, 1875 ; first Cork, first Wolverhampton, first and special cup Maidstone, first Darlington, first Stockton-on-Tees, and champion Crystal Palace, 1876; first Edinburgh, first and cup Swindon, first Blaydon-on-Tyne, first Darlington, first Alexandra Palace, and champion Agricultural Hall, 1877 ; first Wolverhampton, 1878. His measurements are—Nose to stop, 3¾ inches ; stop to occiput, 5¼ inches ; length from occiput to root of tail, 30¾ inches ; girth of skull, 18 inches ; girth of muzzle, 12¼ inches ; girth of chest, 26¼ inches ; girth of loins, 22 inches ; girth of forearm, 6¾ inches ; girth of pastern, 4 inches ; hock to ground, 5 inches ; height at shoulders, 18½ inches.

Nelson was born in the year 1866, and was bred by the well-known Joe Willock. He weighed under 16 lbs., and was by Stokes's Bill out of Willock's Julia. He won first Birmingham, 1868 ; champion prize Crystal Palace, 1871, 1872, 1873 ; first prize Manchester, 1870 ; first and cup Dublin, 1872 ; first Glasgow, 1873.

Before leaving this engaging breed of dog we wish once more to urge upon intending breeders the value of kindness towards their pets. Do not be frightened at him, don't knock him about, or ill-use him, and no dog will treat his master with greater love and respect than will the game, handsome, intelligent, and lovable Bull-terrier.

SCALE FOR JUDGING BULL-TERRIERS.

	Value.
Head	15
Body and chest	10
Feet and legs	8
Stern	2
Colour	10
General appearance	5
	—
	50

THE BULL TERRIER.

OUR modern bull terrier is a very different creature from what he was half a century ago, and I know there are some old "dog fanciers" who prefer the brindled and white and fawn or fallow smut dogs, that were so often kept in our grandfathers' days, to the "milk-white" animals now seen on our show benches.

There is little or no doubt that the original bull terrier was a cross between an ordinary kind of terrier and the bull dog, and some of the largest specimens had a touch of the mastiff thrown in. He had been bred for fighting or for killing rats, and, long before the era of canine exhibitions, some of the rougher so-called sporting men in London and in the Midlands, of which Birmingham may be taken as the metropolis, had strains of more or less celebrity. The dogs that fought with Wombwell's lions at Warwick in 1825 were large bull terriers, and not bull dogs, as stated in the journals of that day, and the fighting dogs of that time and now (for this brutal sport is still followed in many places) were and are bull terriers.

The old-fashioned dog was a much more cumbrous brute than finds favour at the present time, and his colour varied. For instance, James Ward painted one in 1808 that was evidently black and tan, with white on him, a favourite dog of his own, and of a strain highly valued for its courage. This dog had its ears closely cropped, in order, of course, that they might not be in the way of an opponent's teeth when fighting. A little later Marshall painted another bull terrier, black, white, and tan, a dog which the great foxhound authority, Squire Meynell, pronounced to be from one of the best strains he ever knew.

The back numbers of the *Sporting Magazine* contain many representations of the bull terrier, and it is stated that Lord Camelford paid 84 guineas for such a dog, which he later on presented to Jem Belcher, "the Sullivan of those days," for it was but meet that the champion fighting biped should own the champion fighting quadruped. This dog was a fawn or fallow specimen, with legs more or less bowed or crooked, and he was no doubt about equally bred between a bull dog and a coarse terrier.

About this time a dog between 30lb. and 40lb.

was most in favour, few or none of them were altogether white, and brindled or fallow markings of different degrees of darkness on a white ground were commonest.. At the same time there were smaller bull terriers, and these latter were usually used in the rat pit, where their owner's pride lay in an ability to kill a certain number of big rats (we never hear of little rats) within a stipulated time. I think I am quite correct in calling Jemmy Shaw's (London) extraordinary little rat-killer Jacko, a bull terrier, perhaps one fourth bull. This historical creature died in 1869, and amongst other deeds he succeeded in killing sixty rats in 2min. 40sec. ; 100 rats in 5min. 28sec. ; and 1000 rats in less than 100min. ! winning altogether some 200 matches in different parts of the country. These extraordinary feats were performed in 1862-63, and are supposed to be the best on record. Jacko was black and tan in colour, with a little white on his chest, and he weighed 13lb. Again there were even smaller dogs than he, which were kept more for fancy and as pets—still bull terriers, but, for the most part, white in colour.

The popularity of the bull terrier was established fairly enough, and before the era of the fashionable and comely fox terrier, he was no doubt the dog of his day. He could be obtained of any weight ranging between 4lb. and 55lb., and, although in some places he had a reputation for pugnacity, this was more due to his surroundings than otherwise, though those dogs trained to fight in the ring were as savage as savage could be. The typical dog of Bill Sykes, the typical burglar-ruffian, was a bull terrier, a thick heavy-headed creature, with bandy legs, a patch on his eye, and one or two on his body. " William " did not like him all white; a pure dog in colour and reputation would be out of place in such company, and, perhaps for this reason, the more respectable and peaceable member of society, with a fondness for a " game terrier," preferred the entirely white dog; hence its popularity, and possibly the reason why only such came to be looked upon as the genuine article. Still there were others which obtained a better education than the pugilist could give, and they were useful as companions and as watch dogs.

I fancy that most of us at one time or another have owned a bull terrier. The undergraduates at Oxford and Cambridge were fond of him, and at one time it formed as much a part of their equipment as a " top hat " does at the present day. One of the first dogs I ever possessed was a bull terrier, a fawn dog with a black muzzle, and about 30lb. in weight. He was a really good-looking dog, though he cost but half a crown when a month old, purchased from a sporting barber in a country town, whose reputation for dogs was as high as that he possessed as a shaver.

The puppy was christened " Sam," for a long time he was my constant companion, and became an adept at hunting rats by the riverside, a capital rabbiter, and as good a retriever as most dogs. He would perform sundry tricks, find money hidden away, and could be sent back a mile for anything—a glove, a stick—that had been left behind. He would take part in a game at cricket, and fielded the ball so expeditiously that on more than one occasion Sam and I played single wicket matches against a couple of opponents, and as a rule came out success-fully. Altogether this was a kind of dog that could not be obtained now, but on his father's side he came of a fighting stock, and as he grew older he developed a love for a " turn-up " with any passing canines, which caused me to part with him. He was the death of about a couple of dogs, but otherwise he was the gentlest of the gentle ; our cat kittened in his kennel, and with one little shaggy dog be-longing to a friend he struck up a great friendship. Prince, this cross-bred creature's name, was one day turned over and worried by a bully of a sheepdog. In canine language he came and told the story of his woe to Sam. The two set out together, and on our cricket field came across the bully ; Prince and Sam went up to him, the latter, with his tail held stiff and looking savage, seized the sheepdog by the throat, threw him over by a fair buttock in the Cumberland and Westmoreland style of wrestling, then, turning his back on his fallen foe, raised one of his hind legs, and, after treating him in the most disdainful manner possible, trotted off with his little friend.

Poor Sam ! I even now think of him with regret. We had to part, and he was sent to Manchester to do duty as guard in a warehouse and shop. But the smoky Cottonopolis he did not like, nor the confinement ; instead of snarling and barking at the tramps, he "canoodled" with them and made friends —as a watch-dog he was useless. Perhaps he pined for Prince and the cricket. field, for the riverside and the country walks. He died of a broken heart, for he did not like the large town's ways.

This was nearly thirty years ago, and friends of mine still tell me " You never had another dog like Sam," or " Sam was the best dog you ever had." I knew another bull terrier about this period that would jump into the water off the highest bridge that could be found, and, as a set off would put out the flame of a blazing newspaper, or crush a red-hot cinder in his mouth—surely an apt pupil of the "asbestos man," and of the "professor" who dives into a tank from the top of the Westminster Aquarium. But such dogs as these were not show dogs, and, no doubt, shows really made the bull terrier as he is to-day, and caused the almost total extinction of any other bull terrier excepting the white ones. Why white was eventually fixed upon as the correct colour I have already surmised, and as a rule modern specimens breed pretty truly to this hue, though cases of a coloured mark on the eye or on the ear crop up in nearly every litter. Usually such dogs were destroyed at their birth, as being unfitted for success on the bench, though an instance will be mentioned later on where a so-called patched dog did a considerable amount of winning.

To the late Mr. James Hinks, of Birmingham, a noted dog-dealer, who died in 1878, we, in a great measure, owe our present strain of bull terriers. Somehow or other he contrived to get together a strain of white dogs, specimens of which he exhibited with great success at some of the earliest shows, but the very earliest canine exhibitions did not provide classes for bull terriers.

It was early in the fifties that James Hinks began to cross the patched, heavy-headed bull terrier, used for fighting, with the English white terrier, and in due time he produced dogs handsome enough to make a name for themselves, and able to revolutionise the variety. Some of the old " doggy men " said this new breed were soft and could not fight. " Can't they ? " said Hinks, when talking to a lot of his London friends at the Holborn Horse Repository dog show in May, 1862. " I think they can." " Well," said one of the London school, " let's make a match." Hinks, nothing loth, did make a match, and backed his bitch Puss—that day she had won first prize in her class—for £5 and a case of champagne, against one of the short-faced patched dogs similar in weight. The fight came off the same evening at Bill Tupper's well-known rendezvous in Long Acre. It took Puss half-an-hour to kill her opponent, and so little the worse was she for her encounter that she appeared on the bench next morning, a few marks on her cheeks and muzzle being the only signs of the determined combat in which she had been the principal over night. When accounts of this became bruited abroad, although it was not generally believed, the popularity of the " long faced " dog was established. This, however, is somewhat of a digression.

Birmingham in 1864 followed the example of the London committee in providing a class for bull terriers, and it had an excellent entry of twenty-eight. Here Hinks won first prize with Madman, and second with Puss, positions which the same dogs had occupied at Ashburnham Hall, Chelsea, a few months earlier. However, at the latter place the class had been divided for dogs over 10lb. in weight, and for dogs under 10lb. in weight, and a somewhat similar arrangement as to size came to be generally adopted a little later on.

Thus early we find considerable confusion with regard to these bull terriers, solely from the persistence with which their owners stuck to the names of " Madman " and " Puss." Already several bearing both names were shown, and won prizes too, and, although they came to be entered in the first volume of the "Kennel Club Stud Book," no reliance can be placed upon many of the pedigrees published therein. Mr. Joe Walker showed a Puss in 1864, so did Mr. Hinks, and the Stud Book, published in 1874, contains no fewer than twelve bull terriers called " Madman," many of which, I have no doubt, were one and the same animal; and the same volume contains five bitches named " Puss." To separate one from the other, and to verify all the pedigrees, which, as I have said, in many cases were extremely doubtful, would be impossible now.

The dog Madman (2739), which once belonged to the writer, was of a strain distinct from that found in Birmingham, being by a very good old dog of Mr.

Joe Walker's called Crib, from Mr. James Roocroft's Puss. Both these breeders also had white English terriers, with which they had, I fancy, at some time or other crossed the Hink's strain of bull terriers, producing a very nice style of dog, not so heavy and massive as those from the Black Country. This dog Madman was a handsome and companionable creature, and as good a swimmer as ever entered the water. Bull terriers are often good water dogs, and I remember the late Mr. Tom Pickett, of Newcastle, telling me of a bull terrier that he had, I think it was Wallace, a prize winner, which won a swimming match in the Tyne.

Still, dealing with the doubt that clings to the early bull terriers' pedigrees, to further complicate matters the name " Victor " became a fashionable one, and, including a " Young Victor," six such appeared in the first Stud Book, and there are an equal number called " Rebel." We must, however, presume there was but one real " Madman," and that belonged to Hinks ; Dr. Walsh illustrated him in the " Dogs of the British Isles," and he, like all contemporary writers, speaks highly of the sagacity of the bull terrier, and of his adaptability as a companion. He alludes to rough or wire-haired bull terriers, which are, however, of no account, nor ever were ; and there is no doubt that the modern strain is in a great measure due to the animals that sprang from the midland counties, and some few that were bred in the big towns of Lancashire.

The " Madmans," " Pusses," " Victors," and " Rebels " were for the most part large dogs, and for general excellence would compare most favourably with the best specimens seen to-day. I remember some of them very well indeed, as a fact the best of the above at one time or another belonged to personal friends of mine. Were I asked to name the best large-sized bull terrier I ever saw, I should undoubtedly plump for Young Puss, first shown by Mr. G. Smith, jun., of Manchester, who at one time had the strongest team of bull terriers in the country, and later by Mr. W. G. Rawes, Kendal. She was a beautiful bitch in every way, about 40lb. in weight ; one, indeed, with which we could find no fault. She had dark hazel eyes, almond shaped, and not round, a level mouth (which some of our more modern winners have not), and was as handsome a dog as anyone need desire to possess. Born in 1869, she was contemporary with other good specimens, including Victor—old Victor, first belonging to Mr. J. H. Ryder, next to Mr. G. Smith, jun., and afterwards sold to Mr. Cleasby Chorley, of Kendal, with whom he died. Victor was found smothered in his box at the Crystal Palace show in

June, 1872, and it was the writer who first opened that box and discovered the fatality.

As there are some who consider this dog the best bull terrier that ever lived, a line or two may be given him. Victor, who, for a wonder, had no pedigree provided, was a 45lb. dog, with a big head, rather bigger and coarser than I liked—thus I preferred Young Puss to him—a perfectly shaped body, nice dark eyes, good neck and shoulders, and remarkably straight fore legs; in the latter respect, and at the shoulders, he beat any bull terrier I ever saw. He had a well shaped and well carried stern, which was, however, rather coarse. When Mr. Chorley first bought Victor he was a bad-tempered, evil-disposed dog, but in this respect he improved much—whether this arose from the taste for " good ale," which he soon developed, I can scarcely say, but Victor did like ale, and not only would he drink a quart of the beverage, but become intoxicated, and next day evidently ailing with that aching head said to follow a night's debauch, "a glass of bitter" would set the old dog right again.

Following him as a celebrity, came " patched Victor," a white dog with a fawn or brown patch on one ear, a big dog of undoubted excellence, but when the " patch " did not put him out of the prize list some sensation was caused. Whatever truth there might have been in the story that was bandied about relating to this dog, the writer cannot state; but it was said when he won his earlier prize or prizes he was the property of one of the judges who placed him third in priority, and who afterwards sold him for a large sum. As the parties to the transaction have been dead many years, there can be no harm in alluding to what was common report at that time, especially as it gives some little idea of what could occur at dog shows before the Kennel Club had become " so great a power in the land."

Another notable bull terrier of the same date was Rebel (2770), and this dog had likewise belonged to Mr. Smith, jun., and sold by him to Mr. W. H. Akerigg, who turned him over to Mr. Leonard Pilkington, now one of our most popular greyhound coursers. Although Rebel had on occasions beaten Young Puss, to whom he was said to be brother, he was only a second-rate dog alongside her, and inferior to both the Victors already named.

I have mentioned these dogs at considerable length because I believe they were as good as, if not superior to, anything we have at the present time, and when they were in their prime the classes of bull terrier were better filled than is the case now.

I have said the first class at Birmingham had twenty-eight entries; I recollect at one of the Scottish shows (Edinburgh, 1871), there were about thirty-five competitors in the bull terrier classes, and scarcely a bad one in the lot. Now ten or a dozen in a class is considered a first-rate entry, and at Birmingham in 1893, with ten classes and thirty-seven competitors, the group was considered to be an unusually strong one.

So far I have only alluded to the large-sized bull terriers, and what there is to say about the smaller ones is yet to come. After this dog had become fairly well established in the schedules of the shows, the classes came to be sub-divided again, and for many years the classification at Birmingham was for dogs and bitches exceeding 15lb. and below that weight. The competition therein was usually keen, and at this time the names of Mr. S. E. Shirley (the present chairman of the Kennel Club), of Mr. J. H. Ryder, Mr. C. L. Boyce, Mr. J. F. Godfree, Mr. S. Handley, Pendleton, a noted judge, as well as those already mentioned, appeared in the prize lists, and I should say the bull terrier was never so fashionable or had so many admirers as he had, say, between 1868 to 1874. Still he did not bring much money, and from £12 to £25 would have purchased any of the leading dogs of that day, with the exception of the " patched Victor."

Later on, whether bull terriers actually became more valuable, or money was more plentiful, one cannot say, but bigger prices came to be paid for comparatively inferior dogs. One called Tarquin, a ferocious beast, did a considerable amount of winning, and he was one of the high priced division. Then some sort of a longing was apparent for the reintroduction of the patched or marked dogs. Thus classes for bull terriers other than white were provided at one or two of our leading shows, but the specimens shown were not sufficiently handsome to cause the public to fall in love with them. So their continuance was ephemeral, especially as it was very difficult to breed them to type. Lately the very best other than white bull terriers I have seen was one called Como II. belonging to Mr. E. H. Adcock. This was a brindled dog of pretty shape, but heavier and shorter in the head than the modern white dog. I believe that Mr. Adcock's endeavours to perpetuate the strain have not proved successful.

Following the death of James Hinks, of Birmingham, his two sons continued to show their partiality for their father's favourite dogs, and from their kennels many of the modern prize winners have come. For a considerable period Mr. R. J. Hartley, of Altrincham, had a very excellent kennel. His Magnet and Violet, so long as they lasted, monopolised most of the prizes on the show bench, and both were undoubtedly very handsome specimens of their race, as was Mr. A. George's Mistress of the Robes, a daughter of Mr. J. Hinks's old Dutch, who had proved himself almost phenomenal as a sire. The "Stud Book" says Dutch was by old Victor— Champion Countess. Mr. R. J. Hartley, who bred Dutch, tells me that his dam was by Young Gambler from old Daisy, but which Victor sired Dutch is a matter of uncertainty. It was certainly not *the* old Victor alluded to on a previous page as being found dead in his box in 1872. Dutch, in the 1884 "Stud Book," was said to be about six years . old at that time, so his pedigree is doubtful.

With extended classification at shows, and. further alterations therein in the matter of weight, the latter probably brought about by the scarcity of the small-sized bull terrier, good specimens went into more hands. The weights now are arranged as dogs and bitches exceeding 30lb., dogs and bitches between 20lb. and 30lb., and dogs and bitches under 20lb. Thus there is little or no inducement to produce those excellent little dogs of . not more than 16lb. in weight, for such would have little chance of being successful against an equally good specimen half as heavy again. That there is material for re-popularising the breed I am quite certain, and at the last Birmingham show, in November, 1893, several very nice little dogs were shown, at least their character and style were nice, but their crooked fore legs and wide shoulders kept them out of the prize list. Still, the material remains to be improved upon.

Messrs. Lea, of Birmingham, have lately shown some good bull terriers; so has Mr. S. Fielding, of Trentham; whilst Mr. F. North, of Streatham, has been particularly successful, and his Streatham Monarch, which was sold to America for about £80, was certainly one of the best bull terriers of the last year or two. Mr. G. Blair's White Queen (Edinburgh), was likewise another of our very best bull terriers; indeed, I consider these two quite equal to anything we have had since Mr. Hartley's brace, already mentioned. Grand Prior, who has won many prizes, is not deserving of a high place of excellence, solely on account of the fact that his mouth is not level, and for this reason Mr. S. E. Shirley put him out of the prize list at one of the Bath shows. Another celebrated bull terrier whose mouth was not quite level was Mr. Hartley's Magnet. I fancy that, in what I should call the palmy days of bull terriers, a dog with such a malformation would never have been shown, or, at any rate, he would never have attained that high position which Grand Prior appears to have done.

Other modern large-sized bull terriers of more than ordinary excellence have been Messrs. C. and P. Lea's Greenhill Wonder and Faultless ; Mr. T. F. Gibson's Sherbourne King ; Mr. G. H. Marshall's Boston Wonder ; Mr. J. W. Gibson's Bellerby Queen ; Mr. J. R. Pratt's Greenhill Surprise ; Mr. F. Bateson's Lord Gully, Perseverance, and Le Rose ; Mr. R. J. Hartley's Hanover Daisy ; and this list might be considerably extended, though I have probably mentioned the best bull terriers up to date.

Three years ago, the late Jesse Oswell, of Birmingham — a prize-fighter by profession, but a gentleman in nature—had some good dogs, nor must the names of Mr. F. Hinks, Birmingham ; Mr. J. S. Diggle, Chorlton-upon-Medlock ; Mr. James Chatwin, Edgbaston ; Messrs. Mariott and Green, Gloucester ; Mr. J. Rickards, Birmingham ; Mr. J. H. Ryder, Manchester ; Mr. W. J. Pegg, Woodcote, Epsom ; Mr. Firmstone, Stourbridge ; and Mr. C. L. Boyce, be forgotten, as the owners and breeders of choice specimens of this variety. In London, Mr. A. George, a son of the great Bill George, has given much attention to the breeding and exhibition of bull terriers, and between him and Mr. F. Hinks, of Birmingham, must be divided the honour attending the reputation of being the largest dealers in bull terriers in this country.

I have already casually alluded to what must be considered the small variety of bull terriers, such dogs as are under 16lb. weight, and not animals of 25lb. weight starved down until they can be shown in the class restricted to animals not more than 20lb. In our early days of dog shows these little bull terriers were common, and remarkably popular. Now a really good specimen is not to be found, nor will there be any inducement to reproduce such a dog unless the present weight arrangement in dog show classification is changed.

Those who can carry their recollection of bull terriers back for twenty or twenty-five years, no doubt remember such dogs as Dick, Nelson, little Rebel, Triton, Jenny, Kit, Riot, and others shown by Mr. S. E. Shirley; and Mr. Addington's Billy, Mr. J. Willock's Billy, Mr. J. F. Godfree's Napper, Mr. S. Lang's Rattler (a 10lb. dog), and Mr. J. Hinks's Daisy. These were all bull terriers under 16lb. in weight, shapely, well-made, smart, and so far as I can learn, and know from my own ex- · perience, were as game and hardy as any terrier ever bred. Somehow or other they came to languish; the classes provided for them did not fill, and with the result that now stares us in the face, the little bull terrier is no more—at least, he is no more in that perfection of form we saw him on the benches in Birmingham and in London, when **Mr.** Shirley's gallant little dog Nelson ruled the roast.

In 1866 there were twenty entries of bull terriers under 10lb. weight at the London show, and at Laycock's Dairy Yard three years later there were **thirty**-two bull terriers under 15lb. weight against nineteen over that size. Then the former had two classes provided, the latter one class. Now things are reversed, nor can I agree that the fittest survive. Most of these terriers came from the Midlands, Birmingham being responsible for the best of them. Nelson was so bred; but another good one of **Mr.** Shirley's, Dick, had some strains of London blood in him. Unfortunately the pedigrees of these early-date little bull terriers were no more reliable than are those of their larger cousins, and I fancy that they were bred so in and in that they became difficult to rear, and so degenerated. They were never toys, like the small black and tan terriers, and even when crossed with the white English terrier, then more numerous than he is to-day, they maintained their distinguishing character as well as could be expected under the circumstances.

It was always to be much regretted that Mr. Shirley did not endeavour, more than actually was the case, to continue the variety ; and had he done so there is no reason to doubt that the Ettington Park Kennels might now be as noted for "little bull terriers " as they are for wavy-coated retrievers. Could such dogs as Nelson and Dick be produced to-day, I should not be at all afraid of a return to popularity of such a handsome strain.   Messrs. J. F. Godfrey, Hinks, J. Watts, Harry Nightingale, J. Whillock, and E. Bailey, all of Birmingham or the neighbourhood, from time to time had excellent bull terriers under 16lb. in weight, and in their days they brought quite as much money as the larger variety

At one or two of our London shows an attempt was made, similar to what was done with regard to bull terriers other than white, to resuscitate the little dogs by providing classes for them.   The result was, however, a failure, and the one or two competitors were either bandy legged little creatures or indifferent specimens of the English white terrier. So we must take it that for the present the bull terrier under 15lb. weight is lost, and that the illustration on another page is actually out of place in a book supposed to be given over to the description of modern dogs.   We live in times of change and fashion, and maybe another generation may find the restoration of this dog and of the old-fashioned brindled and white, or fallow smut bull terriers of which our "old men" are so fond of talking.

There is no doubt that the bull terrier, be he either big or little, has not reached that height of popularity his merits might deserve, by reason of the obnoxious custom of cropping his ears. This cruelty was originally perpetrated in order that when fighting the ears would not afford hold for an opponent's teeth. Then the aural appendages were cut right off. Now the operation is a much more artistic piece of work, and the ears are so cut as to stand straight up almost to a point, with an inward curve, rather than an outward one, which is said to give the animal a smarter and more aristocratic appearance. It may do so or not, and I cannot deny that a modern bull terrier with his ears on does look, to say the least, dowdy and coarse alongside one that is properly cropped. This, however, arises from the fact that the bull terrier has been bred with ears that will crop the best—thick at the roots, and just such ears that hang badly and look inelegant on the dog that carries them. It would not take many generations to produce bull terriers with nice drop ears, as has been the case with the Irish terrier, which would not require cropping. I have heard it urged that bull terriers never had such good " drop " ears as were sometimes to be found on the original Irish terrier, and that unsuccessful attempts have already been made to breed them with drop ears that would look well uncropped. However, be that as it may, I am afraid that we are a long way off such a desirable change, and the ordinary " bull terrier breeder " is not yet educated up to that point attained by the admirers of Irish terriers ; at any rate, education or otherwise, the cropped bull terrier has not yet had his day. I need scarcely say here that cropping a terrier is illegal, and prosecutions for cruelty to animals under such circumstances have been successful.

This mutilation is usually done when the animal is from seven to ten months old. It is a troublesome performance, requiring considerable skill and nerve. It is customary in many cases to have the dog under chloroform when it is being performed upon, and one operator has an ingenious contrivance to which he fastens the patient with straps. Even when the actual cutting is finished the trouble is not ended, for the ears have to be fastened up, and daily manipulated until they grow into the correct position. Prior to showing bull terriers it is the custom to cut their whiskers, which is again said to smarten their appearance, and the short superfluous hair which grows on the cropped ears is carefully shaved off on the eve of the show. Then it is not unusual to singe the tail in order that it may appear smoother and neater than nature originally made it; and, in fact, a bull terrier is rather a difficult dog to trim and get ready for exhibition, in order that he may appear to the best advantage before the judge.

A few years ago I attended a country exhibition in the North, where there was an excellent class of bull terriers, which the judge had weeded out until only three or four remained. He was about handing the first prize ribbon to a well-known exhibitor, who had charge of a certain dog, which was being shown on a tight chain. Unfortunately the handler inadvertently slackened the chain for a moment, the dog shook itself, and a perfect cloud of white powder flew from his jacket. The judge smiled, the spectators tittered, and the handler, looking foolish, without more ado took his dog out of the ring. Chinese clay was much used on white dogs to hide any yellowness or redness that might appear on the skin, and perhaps also to hide a fawn or brindled mark.

Of course, a dog, even with such an amount of popularity as the bull terrier, could not go long without a club being formed for its improvement, and this came to pass in 1887. The following is a description of the bull terrier as adopted by the Club :—

" *General Appearance.*—The general appearance of the bull terrier is that of a symmetrical animal, and embodiment of agility, grace, elegance, and determination.

" *Head.*—The head should be long, flat, and wide between the ears, tapering to the nose, without cheek muscles. There should be a slight indentation down the face, without ' a stop ' between the eyes. The jaws should be long and very powerful, with a large black nose and open nostrils. Eyes small and very black, almond shape preferred. The lips should meet as tightly as possible, without a fold. The teeth should be regular in shape, and should meet exactly ; any deviation, such as a ' pig jaw,' or being ' under-hung,' is a great fault.

" *Ears.*—The ears are always cropped for the show bench, and should be done scientifically and according to fashion.

" *Neck.*—The neck should be long and slightly arched, nicely set into the shoulders, tapering to the head without any loose skin, as found in the bulldog.

" *Shoulders.*—The shoulders should be strong, muscular, and slanting ; the chest wide and deep, with ribs well rounded.

"*Back.*—The back short and muscular, but not out of proportion to the general contour of the animal.

"*Legs.*—The fore legs should be perfectly straight, with well-developed muscles; not 'out at shoulder,' but set on the racing lines, and very strong at the pastern joints. The hind legs are long and, in proportion to the fore legs, muscular, with good, strong, straight hocks, well let down near the ground.

"*Feet.*—The feet more resemble those of a cat than a hare.

"*Colour.*—Should be white.

"*Coat.*—Short, close, and stiff to the touch, with a fine gloss.

"*Tail.*—The tail should be short in proportion to the size of the dog, set on very low down, thick where it joins the body, and tapering to a fine point. It should be carried at an angle of about 45 deg. without curl, and *never* over the back.

"*Weight.*—From 15lb. to 50lb."

As a matter of fact, I do not think very much of the above description, because of its meagreness and incompleteness, and I am almost afraid that when it was drawn up sundry dogs that had not totally black noses and were somewhat uneven in mouth were occasionally winning prizes. " Over-shot " or " under-shot " mouths, that is where the upper teeth extend over the lower ones, or the lower teeth protrude in front of the upper ones, should be absolute disqualification. This was the creed upon which we were brought up so far as all terriers are concerned, and in bull terriers not the slightest blemish in this particular should be allowed.

The club evidently acknowledges ears cut " scientifically and according to fashion." A bull terrier may have either a small drop ear like a fox terrier; or a semi-erect ear, *i.e.*, one that drops down in front at the tips; or a rose ear, one thrown back, is allowable. However, I am not writing this article as a criticism on the work of the Bull Terrier Club, an acknowledged body of responsible admirers of the variety, who ought to know what they are doing. Perhaps on some other occasion they may improve and modify their code, and be a little more explicit as to what disqualifications are, and how far a " patched dog " is handicapped. At the time of writing this there are marked dogs winning prizes on the bench. I also think they might have said something as to the fawn and fallow and brindled dogs, for such are quite as much bull terriers as the white specimens, though they may not be so fashionable.

The Club does not issue a scale of points, but for the sake of uniformity, and because I do not wish to insult the bull terrier by omitting to do to him what I have done to other dogs, I give him the following tabulation :—

	Value.		Value.
Head, including skull, muzzle, lips, jaw, teeth	25	Neck and shoulders ...	15
		Back	10
Eyes	10	Legs and feet............	15
Ears (badly cropped or otherwise)	5	Coat	10
		Stern	10
	40		60

Grand Total, 100.

Colour, pure white for show purposes; but for ordinary purposes a patched dog, *i.e.*, one with fawn or brindled marks, need not be discarded, nor need fawn or fallow or brindled dogs. The latter are even hardier than the whites, which, whether on account of their colour, or because they are cropped, are often quite deaf. In buying a bull terrier always take care that its sense of hearing is acute. A dog that cannot hear until you pull its tail is no use. One or two very high-class bull terriers in other respects have been almost quite deaf. A notable instance of this is to be found in the dog White Wonder, originally sold as a "deaf dog" to a fancier in America for £80. Evidently not passing muster there he came back to this country, and, shown by

Mr. Pegg at Curzon Hall in 1893, was absolutely disqualified by the judge, Mr. Hartley.

This disqualification caused a considerable amount of sensation and unpleasantness at the time, and it was sought to prove that the dog was not actually totally deaf. Perhaps he was not what is called "stone deaf," but he was about as "hard of hearing" as a white fox terrier I once owned, of which a friend wittily remarked, "it could hear well enough when you rang its tail." Still White Wonder was, in my opinion, sufficiently deaf to justify the action of the judge in the matter.

A very dark hazel eye is desirable, and the small pig-like eyes, with flesh-coloured eye-lids, are to be guarded against. Cherry-coloured or flesh-coloured noses, or parti-coloured noses, should likewise be a severe handicap, if not actual disqualification. The weights ought to be divided—dogs and bitches under 15lb.; dogs and bitches under 30lb.; and dogs and bitches over 30lb. in weight.

Some bull terriers go up to 45lb., or even 50lb., in weight, but such animals are in reality too big, and as a rule when of such a size they lack symmetry, and have more than an inclination to be coarse and heavy in the head. It is one of the most difficult points to achieve in breeding bull terriers, to have them clean and pleasant in the muzzle, i.e., free from anything approaching hanging lips or jowl. Throatiness, too, must be guarded against; indeed, a perfect bull terrier should be as cleanly chiselled or cut in the muzzle, mouth, and neck as a black and tan terrier or as an English white terrier.

In the United States an attempt is being made, or has perhaps in a degree succeeded, to introduce a so-called new variety—the Boston terrier—named after the "hub of the universe." This animal is, from a description I have been given, and from illustrations forwarded me, nothing more than a very bad strain of the old-fashioned fighting bull terrier, and I fancy has nothing to recommend him, still it is being "boomed" in America, and at some shows special classes are provided for him. As is the case with our bull terrier, it is the fashion to have his ears cut.

F. F. Dole's, New Haven, Conn.
GULLY THE GREAT.

THE TERRIER (BULL).

ORIGIN.—This is admittedly a cross between the bulldog and the English terrier.

USES.—Formerly as a fighting dog. Present uses are for vermin, and as a companion it has *no superior*, being kind, gentle, and exceedingly honest and loyal.

* THE VARIOUS PARTS OF THE HEAD, BODY, ETC.

SCALE OF POINTS BY RAWDON B. LEE.

	Value.		Value.
Head, including skull, muzzle, lips, jaws, and teeth .	25	Back	10
		Legs and feet . .	15
Eyes	10	Coat	10
Ears (badly cropped or otherwise) . . .	5	Stern	10
Neck and shoulders . .	15	Total . .	100

GENERAL APPEARANCE.—The general appearance of the bull-terrier is that of a symmetrical animal, an embodiment of agility, grace, elegance, determination, and good nature.

54

HEAD.—Long, flat, and wide between ears, tapering to the nose, without cheek muscles; slight indentation down face, without a stop. Jaws long and very powerful; large black nose, and open nostrils. Eyes small and very black. Lips should meet as tightly as possible, without a fold. Teeth regular in shape, *and meet exactly*, any deviation being a great fault. Ears always cropped for the show-bench, and should be done scientifically and according to fashion.

NECK.—Long, slightly arched, nicely set into shoulders, tapering to head, without any loose skin.

BODY.—Shoulders strong, muscular, slanting; chest wide and deep; ribs well rounded.

BACK.—Short, muscular, but not out of proportion.

LEGS.—Fore legs perfectly straight, well-developed muscles; not "out at shoulder," but set on racing lines; very strong at pasterns. Hind legs long, muscular, with good, strong, straight hocks, well let down.

FEET.—Resembling those of the hare.

COLOR.—White.

COAT.—Short, close, stiff to the touch, with fine gloss.

TAIL.—From 10 to 12 inches long, set on very low; thick where it joins the body, tapering to a fine point; carried at an angle of about 45 degrees, without curl, and never over the back.

WEIGHT.—About 30 pounds.

Mr. J. Lorillard Arden's (44 West 44th St., New York City)
CHAMPION "TOMMY TICKLE"

THE BULL TERRIER

Origin.—This is admittedly a cross between the bulldog and the English terrier.

Uses.—Formerly as a fighting dog. At present it is used for vermin, and as a companion it has no superior, being kind, gentle and exceedingly honest and loyal.

*STANDARD.

General Appearance.—The general appearance of the bull terrier is that of a symmetrical animal, and the embodiment of agility, grace, elegance and determination, strength and courage.

Head.—Long, flat, and wide between the ears, tapering to the nose, without cheek muscles. There should be a slight indentation down the face without a stop between the eyes. The jaws should be long and very powerful, with a large, black nose and open nostrils.

Eyes.—Small and very black, almond shape preferred. Lips should meet as tightly as possible without a fold and not be too deep at the corner. Teeth should be regular in shape, and should meet exactly; any deviation, such as a pig-jaw or being undershot is a great fault.

Ears.—Always cropped for the show bench and should be done scientifically and according to fashion. (Of course this is now obsolete in England).

Neck.—Long and slightly arched, nicely set into the shoulders tapering to the head without any loose skin, as found in the bulldog.

Shoulders.—Strong, muscular and slanting; the chest wide and deep with ribs well rounded.

Back.—Short and muscular, and slightly arched over the loins.

Legs.—Fore-legs perfectly straight with well developed muscles; not out at the shoulder, but set on racing lines and very strong at the pastern joints. The hind legs are long and in proportion to the fore-legs, muscular, with good, strong, straight hocks, well let down near the ground.

Feet.—More resemble those of a cat than a hare.

Color.—Other points being equal, an entirely white dog shall win over one with markings.

Coat.—Short, close and stiff to the touch, with a fine gloss.

Mr. F. T. Miller's (Bay View Kennels, Trenton, Ont.)
"Bay View Brigadier"

Tail.—Short in proportion to the size of the dog, set on very low down, thick where it joins the body, and tapering to a fine point. It should be carried without curl, and never over the back.

Weight.—From 15 lbs. to 50 lbs.

*SCALE OF POINTS.

Symmetry and general appearance	10	Back	10
Skull and jaw	15	Loins	5
Teeth	5	Legs	10
Face	5	Feet	5
Ears	5	Tail	5
Neck	5	Coat	5
Shoulders and chest	15		
Total			100

With the exception of the fox terrier, this is perhaps the most popular of all the terriers that are represented in this country, and each year seems to add new admirers of it. It is certainly one of the most gamy and trim looking dogs, and its generally equable disposition makes it a most desirable companion. There is no question that some fifty years ago this dog was white in color with various colored splashes of red, black, fawn, brown and brindle which accounts for the fact that so many puppies are born with markings as above named, and which of course unfits them for any sort of a record on the show bench. These blemishes, however, are not always transmitted, as proven to-day in the case of Gully the Great, who, notwithstanding that he has a small yellow patch rarely if ever transmits this defect, and which made him so desirable a stud dog years ago. Unfortunately too prevalent is deafness in this breed of dogs, and many an otherwise good dog is barred from the show ring for this cause alone. In fact, some few years ago the fancy was all at loggerheads on account of a famous dog being imported into this country, disqualified for deafness at one of our shows, going back to England and after being disqualified there also, was when the matter was contested declared not to be so deaf as to suffer the before named penalty. Since therefore deafness in whatever degree is to be guarded against in purchasing, this deficiency must be looked for in the puppies, and many of our fanciers destroy those so affected as soon as it is discovered.

The head of the bull terrier is one of vast importance as signalizing the breed. It must be wholly free from cheekiness, as that greatly mars its beauty. A snipy or pinched muzzle, weak jaws, chiselled out before the eyes, light or full round eyes, domed skull, Dudley nose, and uneven teeth are defects in this breed that carry a penalty with them. A short or "throaty" neck is to be avoided, as much so in this breed as in the black and tan terrier. Heavy shoulders or crooked fore-legs are to be eschewed, as is a back that dips behind the shoulders. Weak pasterns, splay feet, and lightness of bone all come under the head of defects.

Though the English demands that the color shall be white, the American standard permits markings, with the understanding that they will count against a dog where a pure white specimen, equal in all respects is competing against him. A heavy tail or a long one, as well as one that is furnished with plenty of hair is always considered as belonging to some other dog than a good bull terrier. The length of the back marks the elegance of the dog, and if it is neither too long nor too short, the desideratum is attained. The ribs should be well sprung.

MISS JAQUET'S BULL-TERRIER CHAMPION FAULTLESS

THE BULL-TERRIER

FEW breeds of British dogs have passed through more troublous times than the Bull-terrier, whose advancement in public favour has been delayed by unknown circumstances. Indeed, it may almost be said that had not the faithful few who have championed its cause through thick and thin possessed a good deal of the indomitable pluck associated with the variety, it would long since have succumbed. In the first place, it must be remembered that the breed has had to live down a very evil reputation—a relic of those days when rat-pit competitions, dog-fights, and badger-baits were common, and regarded as sport not only by the low and the degraded, but by those, for instance, whose higher education was being cared for by their *Alma Mater*. What Oxford sporting undergrad. of half a century or so ago had not heard of Luker's Bull-terriers, or Brakespeare's tubbed badger that had to run the gauntlet of every Bull and other Terrier with sufficient pluck to "face the music" and whose owner could rake up the necessary piece of silver for the "entry"? Or, again, what undergrad. of that period having what was then considered as the true sporting tendencies had not heard of the famous exploits of the riverside Bull-terrier Salter's Dan, a big white-and-fawn, that was about as keen as mustard and a terror on rats and such-like vermin provided by the St. Aldate's and other purveyors for the delectation of undergrads. who "fancied their dogs a bit"? Still more degrading and cruel were the dog-fights that took place in many parts of the country between matched Bull-terriers.

Then followed a somewhat better time for the Bull-terrier—namely, the dog-show era, when the fallow smut, the brindle, and even the patched dog gradually gave way to the smart, white, active dog that we know to-day. The evolution of the all-white dog with his lengthier head and generally smarter framework we owe to the late Mr. James Hinks, of Birmingham, whose sons still maintain the repute for the breed that their father had gained. The troubles of the Bull-terrier fancier did not, however, end with the dawning of the dog-show era and the necessarily considerable increase in the number of fanciers that followed. Being a fighting dog, the ears of

60

the Bull-terrier were subjected to cropping—a process of mutilation that was performed at such a period and in such a way as to be alike brutal and inhuman. This process was continued until comparatively recent times (1895), when it received its death-blow from the Kennel Club. Never by any stretch of the imagination to be called a popular dog, the cropping prohibition tended to make it still less in favour for a few years. However, on every hand now there are signs, and unmistakable ones, that the breed has taken a new lease of life. This is evidenced by the greater number of followers and by the real demand for first-class specimens at remunerative prices. This is matter for congratulation, for as a house-dog and companion a really well-trained Bull-terrier takes a lot of beating; while as a personal guard there is no breed anything approaching it in size that can compare with it.

The Bull-terrier is one of the comparatively few varieties about whose origin there is no mystery. He is mainly Bulldog and Terrier, and it is quite easy to see how, given one of the " patched " dogs that found favour with Bull-terrier fanciers in the old days, and crossing it judiciously with the White English Terrier, Mr. James Hinks succeeded in producing the milk-white variety that we know to-day, and that is more popular in America than with us, despite the fact that our cousins on the other side of the Atlantic have also a Boston Terrier that those who have seen it and are well capable of forming an opinion declare is nothing more nor less than the old fighting Bull-terrier with perhaps slight modifications. In speaking of the constituents from which the Bull-terrier was evolved, only the chief ones have been specifically mentioned—Bulldog and Terrier. Yet there can be little doubt that some of the larger specimens, at any rate, show unmistakable Pointer and Dalmatian blood; while others, again, partake of the Greyhound or the Whippet—and even up to the present day " whippety " is a common expression amongst Bull-terrier breeders for specimens showing affinity to the last-named varieties.

Badger-baiting was common in London about the beginning of the last century, and led up to such disgraceful scenes by drawing the riff-raff of the town together, that the magistrates exerted their power to put an end to the business. This baiting, or drawing, of the badger was a mere worrying of the poor beast in a confined space, and under conditions essentially unfair to him, with dog after dog, until he was torn and exhausted, and was a totally different thing from hunting the badger in his native stronghold.

It may be noted that these degrading practices followed the suppression of bull-baiting in the ring, and naturally so ; for the authorities, in suppressing a practice the public had used as an amusement for centuries, failed to provide opportunities for pleasures of a higher and more rational order. " People mutht be amuthed,"

61

as the lisping showman in "Hard Times," sapiently observed; and the powers that be in this country have scarcely even yet realised the important fact.

Badger-hunting is quite entitled to be called legitimate sport. It is best conducted at night by the light of the moon, when the object is to bag the badger. Late in the evening the badger, which is of retiring and secluded habits, leaves his home to hunt for provender, and in his absence a sack is placed in the entrance to his earth, the mouth kept open by means of a withy bent into a circular form. The dogs are then sent to scour the country round, with the consequence of alarming the badger, which, seeking safety in his stronghold, finds himself trapped at the entrance, the bag being speedily closed, with the "grey" inside, by the party who have been waiting his return.

Terriers are used in digging out badgers, being sent to earth after them, where the dog, if an adept at his work, keeps on baying the badger, thus intimating the position of the quarry to the diggers, who, with ears to the ground, constantly listen that they may know from the sounds where dog and badger have shifted to. It is no easy task for the dog; for the badger, provident against dangers, constructs his earthworks on scientific principles, and has chamber after chamber into which he can retire as he is fought—first out of one and then another. These earths are often constructed among roots of aged trees, and in rocky ground, which makes it difficult for dog and digger combined to dislodge him; and when in light, sandy soil, the badger, borson, bawsind, grey, or brock—for by all these names is he designated—is said to be able to dig his way into new ground as fast as two men with spades can clear the earth to follow him. There is no better dog for badger-hunting than a Bull-terrier, if well entered.

The Bull-terrier, as a breed, seems to have been established towards the end of the eighteenth century. Taplin says: "Terriers have, by the lower classes, for the purpose of badger-baiting, been bred in-and-in with the Bulldog, which has enlarged them and increased their natural ferocity."

Although descended from the dogs referred to, our modern Bull-terrier is much changed for the better, in both appearance and manners. Dog-shows have undoubtedly done much to make the breed respectable, and the well-built, strong, yet active, pure white Terrier, with black eyes and nose, is quite a gentlemanly fellow by comparison with the limping, pied or brindle-and-white, blear-eyed, and face-scarred companions of the Bill Sykes of a past generation.

Mr. W. J. Tredinnick, well known at one time as a breeder of these Terriers, says: "The Bull-terrier, like all other breeds of dogs, has been greatly improved in general appearance, since dog shows have become so general, for now, instead of having a variety of types, colours, and sizes, some of which were far from prepossessing in appearance, we have one recognised type and colour, which has found favour with many gentlemen who would never think of possessing a specimen of the smut, brindle, or patched varieties. The late James Hinks, Birmingham, will long be remembered as one who did more than any other individual to improve the Bull-terrier, and many of our best specimens bear testimony to that fact, as they date from his strain. There are two strains that breeders go back to for pedigree—one known as that of a celebrity called Madman, and the other Old Victor, both of which passed through the hands of the late Mr. Hinks ; but the latter is the fashionable blood of the day."

Although there is a big substratum of truth underlying what Mr. Tredinnick says above, yet the writer is of opinion that classes might very well be provided for " Bull-terriers Other than White," so long as the dogs were typical of the variety. At the present day, however, it is the opinion of the best judges of the variety that if the United Kingdom could be scoured, it would not be possible to find half a dozen Bull-terriers other than white (marked white ones are of course excepted, as there are plenty of those) up to show form.

In reference to colour, it may be observed that the rule to exclude all but white dogs from the prize list has not been absolute. For instance, Young Victor, the son of Old Victor, and the champion dog of his day, had a brindle-marked cheek, and was known as the " patched dog " and the " marked-eyed dog " ; and since his time a similarly marked and excellent Bull-terrier, owned by Mr. Battersby, of Durham, and also named Victor, has won many prizes at North-country shows. Young Victor, the patched dog, was maliciously poisoned at Hull Show, 1877, where he had taken first prize. Other patched dogs that have received awards might also be mentioned.

The pedigrees of Bull-terriers are a subject of confusion which even a Highland seer might be pardoned for failing to unravel. The pedigree of the champion dog Como (K.S.C.B. 19,314) is given simply to point out how meaningless and misleading it is :—

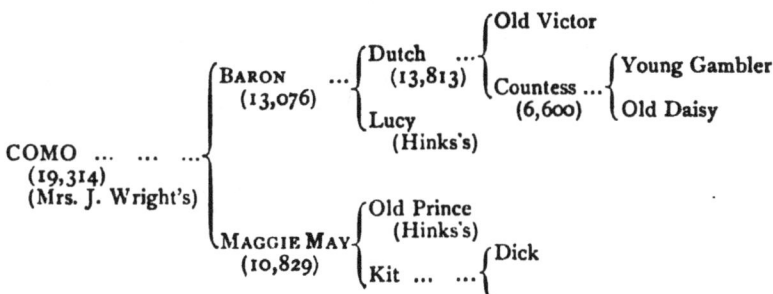

```
                                          ┌ Old Victor
                             ┌ Dutch ...┌─┤
                  ┌ BARON  ..┤  (13,813) └ Countess ...┌ Young Gambler
                  │ (13,076) │                (6,600)  └ Old Daisy
                  │          └ Lucy
COMO ... ... ...──┤            (Hinks's)
 (19,314)         │
 (Mrs. J. Wright's)│         ┌ Old Prince
                  └ MAGGIE MAY┤  (Hinks's)
                    (10,829)  │                ┌ Dick
                              └ Kit ... ...────┤
```

We have Hinks's Dutch (13,813), a bow-legged dog, that was not entered in the Kennel Club Stud Book until he was about six years old, and had won, through his progeny, the prize as best stud dog of his breed, at Aston Show, 1883. The Kennel Club Stud Book gives the age of Dutch as about six years, and his sire as Old Victor. Now, the Old Victor of the Stud Book is No. 2,791, and he died in 1872, six years before Dutch was whelped. The dam of Dutch is, on the same authority, stated to be Hartley's Champion Countess. If this is the bitch entered 6,600 in the Stud Book in Mr. Hartley's name, she was whelped 1874, and is, as given in the table, by Young Gambler out of Old Daisy. Now, there are three bitches named Daisy, all Hinks's property, and bred by him—K.C.S.B. 2,801, 2,802, and 2,803—all whelped in 1866, and out of Old Daisy; and it is highly improbable that the same Old Daisy had a litter in 1866 and another in 1874. Moreover, Daisy (2,801) is said to be by Turk (2,782), and the date of that dog's birth is stated to be 1866, the same year as that of his daughter Daisy—not impossible, but most improbable. Then Daisy (2,802), whelped 1868, is said to be by Hinks's Madman, and that dog is in the Kennel Club Stud Book 2,740, whelped in 1862, and a 15lb. dog, and he had for his great-granddam Old Daisy.

The names Madman, Victor, Prince, Puss, Daisy, occur very often; and as the pedigrees of Bull-terriers are given in the Kennel Club Stud Book, it is often quite impossible to identify the dogs—and, in fact, instead of the clearness and certainty essential to the value of a pedigree, we have a mass of statements alike confusing and contradictory. For the past ten or twelve years breeders of repute have been more particular, and pedigrees are now fairly well kept.

Maggie May's sire may be Hinks's Prince (2,760), a dog that used to be shown as White Prince, and under that name was disqualified at Northampton, as having been castrated, by the late Mr. John Walker and the late Mr. Edward Sandell, as judges—a decision which was confirmed on reference to the veterinary surgeon. The late Mr. Hugh Dalziel believed the sire of Maggie May to be the same dog, as he well remembered, as representative of *The Field*, protesting in that paper against the decision of the gentlemen named, because a minute examination made him certain there was no scar, as there must have been had the operation taken place.

Against the late James Hinks (one of the most straightforward of men) undoubtedly lies a just cause for complaint, for to his carelessness is due, to a considerable extent, the confusion that exists regarding pedigrees.

In the descriptive points of the breed as drawn up by the Bull-terrier Club it may be thought that a very wide margin as regards weight is allowed—15lb. to 50lb. The latter some think far too heavy, as the majority of those dogs belonging to the heavy-weight brigade seem to lack type, sacrificed doubtless by the effort to obtain size. The Club, however, made the minimum 15lb. so as to draw a distinctive line for the "Toys." For some years now the bulk of the specimens at shows have varied between about 25lb. and 50lb. or a little heavier. And though the margin is very wide, it seems to have been brought about by accident rather than by design, owing to the fact that individual specimens of the same litter vary to this extent. The 16lb. or 20lb. Bull-terriers are practically extinct nowadays, and the 25lb. specimens are not much better. It is several years since a good class of "under 30lb." has been seen at any shows; indeed, this class has practically been dropped from the classification of show schedules owing to lack of support.

Mr. Tredinnick many years ago wrote upon the weight question and his remarks thereon may be well worth reiterating at the present moment:—

"Breeders should not go too much for great weight in the large-sized specimen. I consider 45lb. quite large enough for any specimen, especially for exhibition purposes, as when we get above that weight we lose more important details, such as formation of skull, tightness of lip, straight legs, and symmetry—points which should not be sacrificed to get weight. The best sizes for exhibition purposes are 16lb., 20lb., 25lb., and as near to 45lb. as can be. I do not mean to say that a pound or two either way in the large-sized specimens would be objectionable; but the nearer they can be bred to the weights named, the better chance of their success upon the show-bench."

Since cropping was abolished the Bull-terrier Club has worked very hard to settle satisfactorily the "great ear question," and with more or less success; but the ideal ear has yet to be produced. Their efforts have chiefly been directed towards getting the ears as small as possible. It does not matter whether the ears are carried erect or semi-erect, so long as they are small. The "drop" ear does not meet with the approval of Bull-terrier fanciers: it gives the dog a bad expression; but neither this nor any other carriage disqualifies. For show purposes a powerful muzzle and face "well filled up" under the eyes are essential, as the natural ears throw weakness in these points into great prominence.

In selecting a young Bull-terrier, particular attention should be paid to the head. One with a short thick head or showing any tendency to cheekiness is to be avoided. Still, in some strains it is a singular fact that the heads of young puppies are of the "apple" variety. On no less an authority than that of Mr. Pegg the writer has it that the little marked bitch Champion Woodcote Pride, when a young puppy, developed such a plain and ugly head that her breeder was several times on the point of drowning her; in fact, the bitch was only saved by the intervention of his wife. Afterwards the head grew into the ordinary type, and when full grown there never was a Bull-terrier bitch with a better-shaped head. The head should be level and the eyes small and dark (light eyes are a great fault); the fore legs should be straight and the body short. Though in the adult a curl in the tail is a fault, yet young puppies not over teething carry their tails indifferently, and this point need not be too seriously considered in an otherwise promising specimen. As is well known, it was at one time the custom to shave the ears and fine the tails of show Bull-terriers, and this mild form of trimming was allowed by the Kennel Club; but it has since been abolished.

One often sees the character of the Bull-terrier assailed, and this no doubt has in the past acted prejudicially against the breed. In a thirty years' experience with the breed the writer has never fallen across a better breed of game dog that at the same time was capable of a greater degree of affection. With children he has found them perfectly reliable, though he has kept alike the "business" kind and the show-bench modifications of them. That the Bull-terrier will fight, and to the bitter end, if provoked, is perfectly true; but to say that he is, as a breed, of a quarrelsome disposition is a libel. Once a Bull-terrier does really get hold, he is a most tenacious animal, and neither sticks nor kicks nor the usual dodges for separating fighting dogs seem to avail. Some Bull-terriers, despite their scanty coat, make very good water-dogs, while as house-dogs they excel. When cropping was rife, a goodly number of deaf dogs were met with; and it was thought this was a result of unduly exposing a part of a very delicate structure. Other white domestic animals are, however, often deaf—cats, for instance; and Bull-terriers of to-day are frequently deaf.

Some few years ago the Bull-terrier Club made a praiseworthy attempt to produce a pocket edition of the larger animal; but to judge by the comparatively few and indifferent specimens met with, not much success attended their efforts. This is to be regretted, as now that cropping is a thing of the past, a hardy little dog on the lines of the Bull-terrier ought certainly to find a place. Still, the fact remains the Club's efforts were a failure, as they could not get hold of any specimens of the correct type. All the so-called Toy Bull-terriers had apple heads, goggle eyes, and "beaks" like parrots, and altogether were abominations to anyone familiar with a typical Bull-terrier. The writer, in the course of a fairly long experience, can only call to mind two Toy Bull-terriers that were passable, and, writing from memory, these, in his opinion, might just as well have been small White English Terriers.

Below is given a description of the Bull-terrier as furnished by the Bull-terrier Club :—

General Appearance.—The general appearance of the Bull-terrier is that of a symmetrical animal, and the embodiment of agility, grace, elegance, and determination.

Head.—The head should be long, flat, and wide between the ears, tapering to

FIG. 93.—MR. H. E. MONK'S BULL-TERRIER BLOOMSBURY BURGE.

the nose, without cheek-muscles. There should be a slight indentation down the face, without a "stop" between the eyes. The jaws should be long and very powerful, with a large black nose and open nostrils. The eyes should be small and very black, almond shape preferred. The lips should meet as tightly as possible, without a fold. The teeth should be regular in shape and should meet exactly ; any deviation, such as a pig-jaw, or being under-hung, is a great fault.

Neck.—The neck should be long and slightly arched, nicely set into the shoulders, tapering to the head without any loose skin, as found in the Bulldog.

Shoulders.—The shoulders should be strong, muscular, and slanting ; the chest wide and deep, with ribs well rounded.

Back.—This should be short and muscular, but not out of proportion to the general contour of the animal.

Legs.—The fore legs should be perfectly straight, with well-developed muscles ;

67

not out "at shoulder," but set on the racing lines, and very strong at the pastern joints. The hind legs are long and, in proportion to the fore legs, muscular, with good, strong, straight hocks, well let down near the ground.

Feet.—These should resemble more closely those of a cat than a hare.

Colour.—Should be white.

Coat.—Short, close, and stiff to the touch, with a fine gloss.

Tail.—This should be short in proportion to the size of the dog, set on very low down, thick where it joins the body, and tapering. It should be carried at an angle of about 45 degrees, without curl, and never over the back.

Weight.—From 15lb. to 50lb.

To fit the present-day Bull-terrier for the show in the future will not entail quite as much time as was necessary in the ear-shaving and tail-fining days. As, however, he is a muscular dog, good hand-rubbing with plenty of exercise is advisable. The gloss upon the coat, too, may best be acquired in this way, providing the dog be healthy. The washing should take place on the eve of the show, and the dog must then be turned into a well-ventilated kennel plentifully supplied with clean straw. The use of artificial coat whiteners has grown out of a perfectly legitimate practice. When an owner has carefully washed a white dog that he has taken to a show, it is most annoying to find that in transit the animal has soiled his coat. The quickest way to get him clean is to rub on some French chalk and brush it off again. The practice that obtains with some breeeders of smothering their dogs with white powder is a senseless one, and it does no good in any way.

Of those breeders at present before the public who have done great service in endeavouring to popularise this game British dog, Mr. F. Hinks, Mr. H. E. Monk (one of whose dogs is illustrated at Fig. 93), and Mr. W. J. Pegg, may especially be named. The last-named breeder, however, has of recent years given up his very strong kennel of old loves in favour of Bulldogs, though he continues to exercise a desirable watching brief over the Bull-terrier. In the past we have had the late Mr. Alf. George, Mr. J. Oswell, Messrs. Lea, Mr. J. W. Gibson, Mr. Hartley, Mr. B. Garside, Messrs. Marriott and Green, and many others whose names the Stud Books will reveal.

Besides the parent Society, the Bull-terrier Club, there are the Northern Bull-terrier Club and the Birkenhead and Liverpool Bull-terrier Club.

BULL TERRIER—*Ch.* BLOOMSBURY BURGE.

THE BULL TERRIER

WE are so accustomed to associate terriers with sporting functions that the fact of there being no less than six non-sporting varieties may occasion surprise at the first count-up. But if they are not reckoned sporting dogs by the light of the Kennel Club's latest classification, most of them have the sporting instinct well developed, and when you read some of their deeds of derring-do you feel inclined to question their exclusion from the sporting fraternity as much as that of the Great Dane. But as all marriages ought to be made in heaven, so all canine classification ought to be, and is, decided in Grafton Street, and the elders and betters of the dog-fancying world have decreed that the bull terrier, the black and tan, or Manchester terrier, the English white terrier, the miniature black and tan terrier (heretofore known as the "toy terrier"), the Clydesdale terrier, and the Yorkshire terrier shall be accounted dogs outside the sphere of sport, and for one of them—the English white terrier—have thrust it out from the privileges of registration altogether, whereby it has no legal claim for recognition in these pages. But since it survived into the twentieth century, and since it is a good old English breed—as age goes in modern dogs—only fallen on evil days, and since it still has lots of friends, I am not going to give it the cold shoulder although it has been disenfranchised.

I will now proceed to deal with these six non-sporting terriers in the order given, albeit it departs from the alphabetical system I have hitherto observed, but some of these breeds appear to " pair off," and are most conveniently dealt with in conjunction with one another, as, for instance, the Manchester and the English white

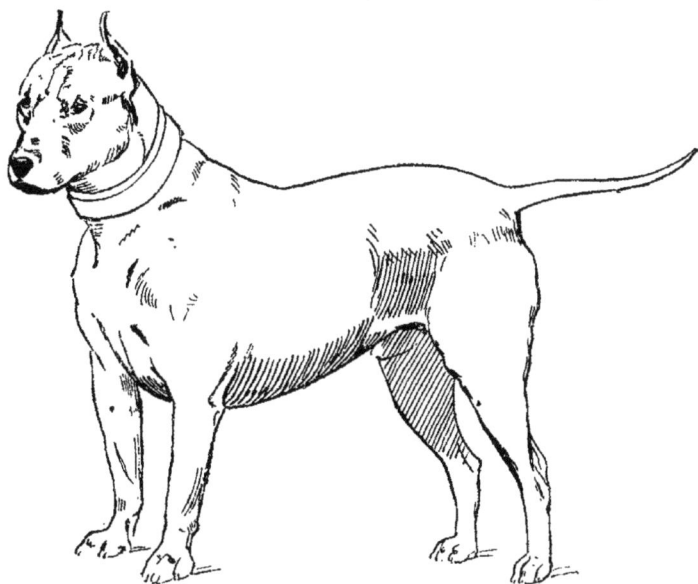

BULL TERRIER (Before the Anti-Cropping Edict).

terriers, the Clydesdale and the Yorkshire, which are respectively of kindred types. Whilst the bull terrier, with which I begin, stands a head and shoulders above, and may attain to double and even treble the weight of the largest of the other five members of the family.

The bull terrier is a dog that has had its hey-day. At one time it stood the chance of making a great position for itself in life, and somehow missed it. A fairly modern breed—its earliest records do not extend farther back than the last reign — it achieved an undeniable fashion about the middle of the Victorian era, and men under fifty can remember how in the third quarter of the last century the bull terrier was reckoned perhaps the most desirable canine adjunct, and in certain circles went hand in glove, as it were, with a university education in giving proper sporting tone to gilded youth ; but that was before the vogue of the bulldog had penetrated into the most aristocratic society.   The bull terrier had many striking qualities, he was " pallish " and faithful, marvellously game and plucky, a splendid ratter, and a dog that ever wanted a fight, and to a finish.   You saw it oftener at the respectable heel than any other dog, and, whilst it occasioned a cult amongst professional fanciers, it was also highly popular with all and sundry.

The bull terrier of to-day is a varmint-looking fellow, who has, in the last thirty years, sloughed off his coat of patched colour and appeared in the immaculate purity of all white.   He has lost none of his gameness, and is " all there " from snout to stern, with his little, black, wicked, oblique eyes glinting for a problematical puss, a derelict rat, or a fortuitous fight.   He rings the changes of every weight from a " toy " under 12 lbs. (he has been known to fail the scale at half that number) to a solid fighting force of considerably over 50.   I doubt not that in our northern counties you shall still find specimens worthy to emulate the heroic deeds of the famous *Jacko*, who (as Mr. Rawdon Lee has recorded) was altogether a famous little spirit of his times.   He was black and tan in colour, with a little white on his chest, weighed 13 lbs., and starred the country, winning some 200 rat-killing matches, his principal achievements being 60 rats in 2-40, 100 rats in 5-28, and 1000 rats in less than 100 minutes! These prodigies of valour and activity were performed in the early 'Sixties, and constitute records for the rat-pit.

As its name indicates, the bull terrier is a manufactured breed, derived, some say, from a cross between the bulldog and the old English white terrier. It is also asserted to contain in its veins a distant strain of hound, greyhound, pointer, and mastiff blood; but as this statement comes to us by way of America (where they have annexed its prototype and called it a "Boston terrier"), it does not occur to me as more correct than the illustration given of a "typical" bull terrier in the shape of an animal with a body as long as a racing hound's. I merely mention it to indicate the unsuspected extras those who contemplate going in for this breed may hope to get for their money. Howsoever its type is come by, the modern result is satisfactory, both in the spirit and in the flesh, and its lovers can only regret this is not more appreciated by the current generation. And I prefer to give prominence to the notes and opinion of Mr. C. Hopwood, the well-known specialist judge of this variety, who writes—

The type of the bull terrier to-day is as good as it ever was, and would be even better than it is had not the Kennel Club's ruling prohibited cropping. This has undoubtedly had the effect of causing the breed to lose some of the popularity it enjoyed years ago. But it is now gradually regaining its old place, and if those who own the breed will bear in mind that the bull terrier should have very little lip, and no appearance of being leggy, the breed should go on in a way satisfactory to everybody. My love for the breed has remained firm for over thirty-five years, and reached its height when I became associated with Ch. *Como*, a dog whose disposition and gameness were only equalled by its physical perfection. The only addition I should like to see made to the modern bench would be some good small ones, such as *Kelpie*, whom I considered the best light-weight bull terrier I ever saw

He was owned by a friend of mine, who sold him to a gentleman who kept Bedlingtons, and wanted "a game dog about 16 lbs. weight." He went to that gentleman, with the guarantee that "he would take his death with anything." Three days later that gentleman wrote to my friend, asking him to take *Kelpie* back, as "he had already killed two of his Bedlingtons, and he was beginning to grow suspicious of him." Mr. Hopwood goes on to say that as a companion there is no dog alive equal to a bull terrier, especially in towns and cities, where there is little room. He deplores the scarcity of good judges, and those misguided experts who "go in for long-legged specimens, with lips like pointers."

Mr. Frost, the Honorary Secretary of the Northern Bull Terrier Club, considers that the chief difficulty in the breed is "getting it to last, some strains having a tendency to go thick in the skull. Perhaps another dash of white English terrier might remedy this defect"; Mr. J. D. Dudson, the late owner of the excellent specimen that illustrates this article, is of opinion that "some breeders, to get the bull terrier's ears lighter, have been breeding with the English white terrier, and getting the breed too fine. We want a short, cobby body, good square jaw, tight lip, and plenty of bone. By crossing with the English white terrier you lose bone, and, above all, square muzzle and fighting lines."

The rule prohibiting cropping was a severe blow to the breed, but the specialist clubs accepted it in a loyal spirit, and few can find fault with the lightly-carried, thin-textured ears of *Bloomsbury Burge*. The disability to crop has, as a consequence, completely changed the character of the ear. Formerly a good solid quality of leather was wanted ; it was stronger, and, when cropped, much easier to "set" than a thin ear. The ears which have now been developed are, in many leading dogs, positively too small to cut, and so thin and lightly carried that they do not take off from the length of the dog's face, as was the case when, directly after the edict against cropping, there were only thick, heavy-eared dogs in the breed.

"The cropping edict," writes Mr. Frost, "has undoubtedly done the breed a lot of harm, and had it not been for the existence of the specialist clubs would probably have had a fatal effect on the fancy. But we, as a body of specialists, realising the great amount of influence that had been brought to bear on the Kennel Club to compel the legislation, adapted ourselves to the new regulations with a determination to keep the noble breed alive, and to that end gave all club special prizes to uncropped specimens, which had the effect of getting the classes well filled. But it cannot be denied that the bull terrier has lost a good deal of his smart, business-like appearance, and the discontinuation of cropping probably accounts for the present-day dog looking 'cheeky,' as no doubt it took a lot of strength from the cheek muscle to get the ear erect. Unfortunately the troubles of the breed have not ended with the cropping question, as the Kennel Club in its wisdom has seen fit to abolish the trimming of bull terriers' tails for exhibition purposes. This was not a cruel practice ; it was always done openly, and with no intent to deceive, and it greatly enhanced the look of the dog. And if a poodle may be clipped, it passes comprehension to understand why a very modified form of the same treatment should be illegal in the bull terrier."

Mrs. Elizabeth Kipping, who owns *Delphinium Wild*, one of the best bitches in the breed, would like to see the modern dog a little larger, and with more bone than it possesses at present. She considers that " their extreme terrier quality, with their small, dark, oblique-placed eyes, sets them in the front rank of the terrier family," and finds them "splendid guards. Like the bulldog they seldom bark, but, when occasion requires, are a terror to the unwelcome guest." And winds up with this pleasant and simply-told little anecdote :—

I was walking with *Wild Rose*, the dam of *Delphinium Wild*, near some ponds in Epping Forest, when one of a number of children playing on the bank fell into the water. *Wild Rose*, entirely of her own accord and instinct, immediately jumped in and brought the child ashore. I think that alone would endear the breed to any one.

I am sure there will be many to echo the sentiment, " Well done, *Wild Rose !* "

Mr. Charles Hopwood of Manchester, one of the oldest dog-fanciers, and most popular in the north of England, sends me the following description :—

MR. CHARLES HOPWOOD'S IDEAL BULL TERRIER.—My " ideal" bull terrier should have the head long, flat, moderately wide between the ears, good, broad, powerful under jaw, free from lippiness ; large, black nose ; well-filled-up foreface ; small, dark eyes, not set wide apart ; ears small and semi-erect in carriage ; neck long, and set well in the shoulders ; chest wide and deep ; nice short back, with muscular loins ; and the best of legs and feet, with plenty of bone. The colour should be white, but a lemon patch on the side of the face is not objectionable if other qualities are good. The tail must be short, set low, and carried well down, below the level of the back.

I append the Standard of Points as given by the Bull Terrier Club of Scotland in rather more detail than in the Northern Bull Terrier Club's book. Both these institutions foster the breed in the north of Britain, where it seems more popular than in the southern counties. The entrance fee for the Northern Bull Terrier Club is 5s., and the annual subscription 10s. 6d., and the Honorary Secretary is Mr. J. Frost ; the same entrance fee, but only a subscription of 5s., is levied from the members of the Scottish club, whose headquarters are at Glasgow, and the Honorary Secretary Mr. Green. A third kindred institution is the National Bull Terrier Club.

STANDARD OF POINTS OF THE BULL TERRIER

The GENERAL APPEARANCE of the bull terrier is that of a fine-balanced, compact, symmetrical animal, with a combination of great strength, grace, alertness, and determination.

The HEAD must be long, flat, and wide between the ears, tapering to the nose, which is very large and black, with wide open nostrils. Cheek muscles not exaggerated, nor showing distinct bumps like the bulldog, but evenly distributed and merging imperceptibly into the muzzle. There should be a slight indentation down the face without a "stop" between the eyes. The jaws, one of the most important points in the breed, must be long and very powerful, not square nor snipey, but presenting a circular appearance, and filled right up under the eyes, with a resolute and well-marked under jaw. Eyes very small, very black, almond-shaped, or with a triangular setting. The lips must meet closely without loose skin, and not too deep at the corner. The teeth are large, strong, and regular in shape, the top fitting tightly over the bottom; any deviation, such as "pig-jaw," or being "under-hung," is a great fault.

EARS must be small and carried semi-erect.

The NECK must be long and column-like, set firmly and squarely into the shoulders, but with no loose skin, as found in the bulldog.

The SHOULDERS must be strong, muscular, and slanting; chest wide and deep, expressive of power and grace.

The BACK must be short and muscular, and slightly arched over the loin. Ribs, barrel-shaped and close together, with well-developed inter-costal muscles. Loins very short, hard and compact, well tucked-up, with, however, no approach to a whippet outline. Long backs, with a dip behind the shoulders and weak loins, are greatly to be condemned.

The LEGS must be straight and hound-like, with plenty of good round bone, very strong at the pastern joints. The thighs are somewhat long, with big muscles, short straight hocks, and springy movement.

The FEET are of the cat pattern, well knuckled, toes close together, with strong pads, and stout short nails.

COLOUR should be white; but slight markings, although a blemish, do not disqualify.

The COAT must be short, close and stiff to the touch, with a fine gloss.

The TAIL must be very short, set on low, thick at the root, and tapering to a fine point. It should be carried perfectly straight, without a curl, and at no time higher than the level of the back.

WEIGHT from 12 to 60 lbs. Toys under 12 lbs.

FAULTS.—Small pig-like eyes, with flesh-coloured lids; Dudley or butterfly nose; lippiness and throatiness.

My illustration represents Ch. *Bloomsbury Burge*, late the property of Mr. Dudson. It was bred by Mr. Monk, the sire being Ch. *Bloomsbury Prince* and the dam *Bloomsbury Grace*. *Burge* stands about 17 inches at shoulder, weighs 48 lbs., and is all white in colour. He has tremendous length of head, well-finished ; great strength of muzzle ; well-developed under jaw, and a big, black nose. His eye is perfect as to shape and colour, with good, hard, keen expression. His body, legs, feet, and shape are as good as they can be, and he possesses enormous bone, and particularly excels in the carriage of his tail. The photograph was snapped just as he was about to spring off the table, and his body is too much extended, for he is very cobby in build. He has won six championships, including the K.C. 1903, twenty-one firsts, and many lesser prizes.

T THE beginning of the nineteenth century we have the first information regarding the cross of the bulldog on the terrier, though there is no reference to the outcome as being anything but simply terriers until about 1820. In the first volume of "Annals of Sporting," published in 1822, there is an article accompanying a picture of a black-and-tan smooth terrier bitch and a patched bull terrier. Pierce Egan, a celebrity as a sporting writer, and whose command of new sporting words and phrases would make our entire army of baseball reporters turn green with envy, was the first to draw attention to the breed. It is too long an article to quote in its entirety, so we condense as follows:

"The Tike most prominent in our view is of that variety, now an established one, which a few years since passed under the denomination of the Bull-Terrier; the bitch [the smooth black and tan] is intended for a full-bred terrier. . . . We are not aware of any new *dub* for the half-bred bulldog, our present theme, or any substitute as yet, for the term Bull-Terrier. This deficiency, if such it be, is preferable to a congress of the Fancy, or, perchance, to chance medley, another notable instance of *ton*. The new breed is, beyond question, admirably well adapted to the purpose of a companion and follower to the *Swell* of either description, whether a *walking jockey*, or one mounted. . . . To return to *"elenchi"* or rather, the Bull-Terrier, back again, he is a more sprightly and showy animal than either of the individuals from which he was bred, and equally apt for, and much more active in any kind of mischief, as it has been well expressed. . . . The true bred bulldog is but a dull companion and the terrier does not *flash* much size, nor is sufficiently smart or *cocking*, the modern mixed dog includes all of these qualities, and is of a pleasant airy temper, without losing any of the fierceness, when needed, of his prototypes; his colours, too, are gay and sightly. . . . Much depends, with respect to the *flash* appearance of the dog under notice, on the management of his head and stern during his early puppyhood. By this we shall readily be understood to refer to his ears, which must, at all events, in order to his coming to a good place, have the true, upright, pricked, *kiddy* crop, and in the next place he must be *nicked* in that workmanlike style, which shall produce an alternative elevation and depression of his stern, in exact agreement with the model we have exhibited.

"We have been, however, performing a work of supererogation, not at all necessary to our sporting salvation or flash repute, in varnishing the new breed, which has become so truly the go, that no *rum* or *queer kiddy*, or man of *cash*, from Tothill Street in the West to North-Eastern Holloway, far less any swell *rising sixteen*, with a black, purple or green Indiaman, round his *squeeze*, the corner of his variegated *dab* hanging from his pocket, and his pantaloons well creased and puckered, but must have a tike of the new cut at the heels of himself or *prad*."

The first book pertaining to dogs to refer to the bull terrier by a name and give it a chapter is Captain Brown's "Anecdotes of Dogs," published in 1829. His description is of the early crosses.

"He has rather a large, square head, short neck, deep chest and very strong legs. He possesses great strength of jaw and draws a badger with much ease. He is of all colours, and often white, with large black or brown patches on different parts of his body. His hair is short and stiff." It is very evident that Captain Brown got most of the rest of his chapter from Egan's sketch, but in Brown's chapter on the Scotch terriers he says that the cross between the leggy fifteen-inch Scotch terrier and the bulldog made the best bull terrier. Stonehenge also mentions this cross in his first edition, but said they were not so game as the smooths.

To Captain Brown we are also indebted for the following original anecdote which Sir Walter Scott sent to him: "The wisest dog I ever had was what is called the Bull-dog Terrier. I taught him to understand a great many words, insomuch that I am positive that the communication betwixt the canine species and ourselves might be greatly enlarged. Camp once bit the baker, who was bringing bread to the family. I beat him and explained the enormity of his offence, after which to the last moment of his life, he never heard the least allusion to the story, in whatever voice or tone it was mentioned, without getting up and retiring into the darkest corner of the room with great appearance of distress. Then if you said 'The baker was well paid,' or 'The baker was not hurt at all,' Camp came forth from

OLD DUTCH

Fred Hinks' great sire, a pillar of the Stud Book

VENOM

Published in 1831 in the "Sporting Magazine"

SIR WM. VERNER'S TARQUIN

Shown at New York in 1880

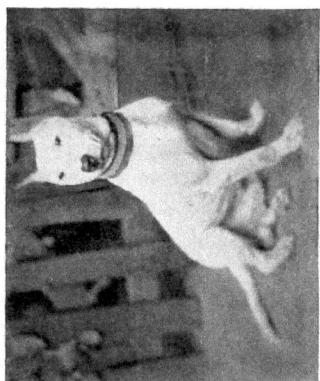

CHAMPION MAGGIE MAY

One of Mr. Frank Dole's old winners and producers

PRESIDENT and VICTORIA

Two early importations shown by the late E. Sheffield Porter

BRUTUS

Painted by Edwin Cooper and published in the "Sporting Magazine"

his hiding place, capered and barked and rejoiced. When he was unable, towards the end of his life, to attend me when on horseback, he used to watch for my return, and the servant used to tell him his master was coming down the hill or through the moor, and although he did not use any gesture or explain his meaning, Camp was never known to mistake him, but either went out at the front to go up the hill, or at the back to get down to the moor side. He certainly had a singular knowledge of spoken language."

What the bull terrier of that period resembled we show by reproductions of some prints, published from 1820 to 1830. The badger drawing by Alken is a fancy sketch, but he was a first-class reproducer of sporting scenes of this character, and in all probability the participants are portraits of well-known sporting men of the day, so we may accept the dogs as being typical. The black markings near the tails on both dogs suggest fox terriers as much as bull terriers, but they are of the same type as the illustration Pierce Egan wrote the description for, that drawing being also by Alken. For that reason we place this with the bull terriers. Of the other two engravings there is no doubt whatever, and that of Venom is surprisingly good. Her short tail indicates the bulldog cross, which is much more apparent in the portrait of Brutus, from a painting by Edwin Cooper.

Birmingham was the city where the show bull terrier was brought to perfection. The most of the good imported dogs have been from that district, and the largest exporter to this country is Fred Hinks of that city, whose father was also a bull-terrier breeder for many years. Bull terriers in England got a hard set-back when the anti-cropping rule of the English Kennel Club went into effect a few years ago, and to the eye of any person accustomed to the cropped dog those with natural ears look soft, cheeky and anything but the smart bull terrier of the old days. Old fanciers gave the breed up, and although there are some signs of revival, it is uphill work, with ears of all sorts as to shape, size and carriage. Bloomsbury Burge is claimed to be about the best dog in England now, and our readers can see what a good uncropped bull terrier looks like from his photograph. Even if the Englishmen still had their dogs cropped they could not show classes at any show the equal of our annual New York display. We do not claim that our best dog will always be a better one than the best English dog, but we can show more good American-bred bull terriers at New York than are shown throughout the whole of England in the entire year. It is the old story of breeding more, and therefore having more to select from.

The first bull terriers of class shown in America were the pair Sir William Verner sent over in 1880 for exhibition at New York. These were Tarquin and his son Superbus. Tarquin was the best dog in England at that time, or one of the best, and had won more prizes than any dog then being shown. He was a large-sized all-white dog, and it was a long time before we saw his equal in this country. Mr. Mortimer had two or three that he was showing at that time, and he was the most successful of our exhibitors till Mr. Frank Dole took up the breed, for whom we bought his first bull terrier when in England in the winter of 1884. This dog he called The Earl, and he won in New York the next year and was sold to Mr. C. A. Stevens. Mr. Dole then went in for quite a series of purchases, his first good dog being Count, with which he won a number of prizes; then came Jubilee and White Violet, followed by the prominent English winning bitch Maggie May, the dam of that wonderful bitch Starlight, who was able to win even when she had hardly a front tooth left, taking first in winners at New York, in 1899, when nearly twelve years old.

A good many of the imported dogs of this period were by a dog called Dutch, usually spoken of as Old Dutch. He was never shown, as he was all wrong in front, but he was a remarkable good-headed dog, as is shown in the photograph we reproduce. One of his best sons was Grand Duke, imported by the Livingston Brothers, and this dog was the sire of Starlight. There was no lack of competition at the time these dogs were being shown, for Mr. W. F. Hobbie and the Retnor Kennels had some good ones, the former showing Spotless Prince and Enterprise with success, the latter having Diamond King and Dusty Miller. Diamond King was the first of the get of the great sire Gully the Great to come to this country, and later on Gully himself was imported by Mr. Dole. Mr. John Moorhead, Jr., of Pittsburg, was the next new exhibitor to make a stir, as he won in the open class and also took the breed special with Streatham Monarch in 1892, but he failed to do anything with the puppies of his own breeding.

Gully the Great made his first appearance at the New York show of 1893, and was placed second to the American-bred Young Marquis, which was a Dole-bred dog, being by Bendigo out of Edgewood Fancy, who was out of Starlight. Edgewood Fancy is the first with the prefix which Mr. Dole has rendered very much akin to a hallmark, and the Edgewoods have had a long and honourable record of wins since that time. Carney and Cardona were the next two important arrivals from England, and both

MODESTY

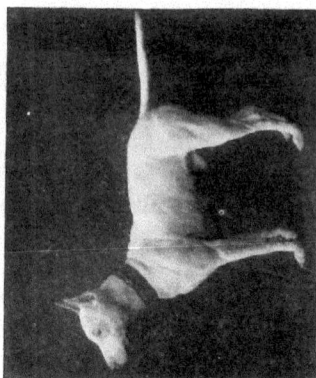

CHAMPION PRINCETON MONARCH

CHAMPION CARNEY

WENTWORTH BRANT

DICK BURGE

EDGEWOOD PENN

84

were by Gully the Great. Dr. Rush S. Huidekoper bought Cardona soon after he came out and showed him successfully for several years. He was a very good dog and lasted well.

The next dog of eminence was Princeton Monarch, shown by W. & L. Gartner. Although not always successful, he had a long list of wins to his credit, and even when seven years old he was able to take first in winners at New York in 1904 under the English judge, Mr. W. J. Pegg. His great rival was Woodcote Wonder, which Mr. Dole imported, and for some time it was nip and tuck between them, but Wonder finally seemed to get settled in first place and held it until he went to California, where he remained for a year or two, only to be purchased by the Bonnybred Kennels of Brooklyn for stud purposes.

Among other former exhibitors the late Frank H. Croker was one of the leaders about five years ago. Fire Chief was one of his best dogs, but he had a better terrier in the bitch Yorkville Belle. Mr. H. F. Church is another who has been prominent, more particularly with lightweight terriers, his Little Flyer being almost invincible at his weight, and from him came a number of good dogs. Mr. Church is still exhibiting. Mr. James Conway was another who showed some terriers that were winners, but he went in for bulldogs and sold out his terriers to Mr. Arden. Dick Burge, Modesty and Southboro Lady were three he owned. James Whelan, of New York, is another of the old fanciers, and he had much to do with Mr. Croker's success. Guy Standing, William Faversham, Mark O'Rourke and James Parker have had some prize winners that made good records, and Tommy Holden is getting to be one of our "oldest exhibitors," though he does not look the part by any means. Nor must the Bay View Kennels of Canada be omitted, Mr. Miller having owned and bred many winners shown with that prefix. Time of course makes changes in the list of exhibitors, and at the present date we have to add to those already named who are still exhibiting Mr. Clair Foster, J. W. Britton, 2d, Elm Court Kennels and Isaac H. Clothier, of Philadelphia.

The bull terrier is one of the breeds in which America holds its own, and one of the most surprised persons at the New York show in 1904 was the English judge, Mr. Pegg. He told us when we got through his judging of bull terriers and bulldogs that the former gave him the hardest task he had ever had in the judging ring. Not only were the classes large, but they exceeded anything he had ever seen for the number of sound, good dogs. We noticed in Mr. Pegg's judging that he did not favour length of head or muzzle, but dogs that showed strength; went for the type that Vero Shaw used to show when he was the leading exhibitor in England years ago.

There has been an inclination on the part of many judges to select a dog too high on the leg for the proper type of bull terrier. The correct thing is a dog showing substance and strength, with a punishing jaw. The standard says that the skull should be widest "between the ears," which is ridiculous, for the ears are well up on the skull. The formation of the head is slightly oval, or looks so owing to the muscle on the cheek, but as little of cheekiness should appear as possible. The set of the eyes is peculiar, as they are or should be rather close together and set obliquely, black and small. The fore face shows no drop below the eyes nor the muzzle any snipyness. The latter should be carried well out to the nose, and in profile the under jaw should show strength. Teeth strong, devoid of canker and meeting evenly in front. Lips showing no hang, other than sufficient to cover the teeth. The bull terrier is the widest dog in front of any of the terriers, not out at elbows but wide because of the width of brisket. A short back is imperative in this breed, with plenty of chest room and short, strong loin. The hind quarters should show great strength and power, with the second thighs well developed. The standard we give is that in Vero Shaw's "Book of the Dog," and our reason for selecting that somewhat out-of-date publication is because Mr. Shaw was, as we have already stated, a leading bull-terrier exhibitor and had a better knowledge of the breed than any person of his day or any writer since then. A word is perhaps necessary to explain the term "moderately high" with reference to the fore legs. Fox terriers and all, with the exception of the Irish terrier, were decidedly cobby compared with our terriers. We know the type of terrier he had and wanted. Some of our readers may recall Mr. Mason's Young Bill; if they do, then they will know the type of dog Mr. Shaw meant when he wrote his description.

Descriptive Particulars

Head.—Should be flat, wide between the ears and wedge shaped; that is, tapering from the sides of the head to the nose; no stop or indentation between the eyes is permissible, and the cheek bones should not be visible.

RANCOCAS GINGER
Property of Mr. H. Tatnall Brown

EDGEWOOD J. P. II.
Property of Mr. W. Freeland Kendrick

CH. FAULTLESS OF THE POINT
Property of Mr. Clair Foster

CH. BLOOMSBURY BURGE
A specimen uncropped English dog

CH. EDGEWOOD CRYSTAL
Formerly the property of Mr. F. F. Dole

CH. AJAX OF THE POINT
Property of Mr. Clair Foster

Teeth.—Should be powerful and perfectly regular—an undershot or overhung mouth being very objectionable—and the lips thin and tight; that is, only just sufficient to cover the teeth, and not pendulous as in the bulldog.

Nose.—Large, quite black, and damp, with the nostrils well developed.

Eyes.—Must be small and very black. As regards shape, the oblong is preferable to the round eye.

Ears.—Are almost invariably cropped and should stand perfectly upright.

Neck.—Should be moderately long and arched, free from all trace of dewlap and strongly set upon the shoulders.

Shoulders.—Slanting and very muscular, set firmly on the chest, which should be wide.

Fore Legs.—Should be moderately high and perfectly straight, and the dog must stand well on them, for they do not, as in the case of the bulldog, turn outward at the shoulders.

Feet.—Moderately long and compact, with toes well arched.

Body.—Deep at chest and well ribbed up.

Hind Legs.—Long and very muscular, with hocks straight and near the ground.

Coat.—Short and rather harsh to the touch.

Colour.—White.

[Mr. Shaw was strongly opposed to any marked dogs, and we agree with him on this point. The practice of giving prominent places at shows to marked dogs is increasing and should be stamped out. To our mind a patch is as much a disfigurement on a bull terrier as a white breast spot on a black-and-tan terrier.—ED.]

Tail.—Fine, set low, and not carried up, but as straight from the back as possible.

In general appearance the bull terrier is a symmetrical dog, apparently gifted with great strength and activity, and of a lively and determined disposition.

SCALE OF POINTS

Head	30	Colour	20
Body and chest	20	General appearance	10
Feet and legs	15		
Stern	5	Total	100

BULL TERRIERS.

WE have but little authoritative information as to the origin of this breed, which appears to have been established towards the end of the eighteenth century. There is, however,

* The bat ear is absolutely erect and is rounded at the top, whilst the tulip ear is erect at the base, with the tip more pointed and falling with a forward bend.

no doubt that the first cross was made between the Bulldog and the Terrier, and the cross-bred progeny were called "Bull-and-Terrier" or the "half-bred" dog; other blood such as that of the Greyhound, Pointer and even Dalmatian has in time past also been introduced, traces of which can still be observed in the character and marking which now and again reappear.

"DUTCH."

ONE OF THE GREATEST STUD DOGS OF THE PAST.

The present type of dog has doubtless been in great degree obtained by the crossing of the Bulldog with the white English Terrier, and by selection of those specimens which showed most of the Terrier type, whilst still retaining the courage of the Bulldog, to breed back again with the

Terrier. The not infrequent brindle, fallow and other markings still attest the presence of Bulldog blood.

There is little doubt that the dog, in the first instance, was bred especially for courage, activity and general staying power with a view to pit fighting, badger-baiting and other such like pastimes; for we first hear of the dog (in Birmingham and the Black Country) about the middle of the last century, or, may be, a little earlier, at which period these forms of sport were greatly in vogue. The Bulldog was doubtless chosen for his undeniable courage and tenacity of grip and the Terrier for general activity and staying power. The offspring from such a direct cross would be far too thick set; and this probably necessitated further crossing in order to reduce the Bull strain. To obtain larger dogs other breeds were evidently resorted to which accounts for the characteristic signs previously mentioned.

The description of the breed, as drawn up by the Bull Terrier Club, is as follows :—

DESCRIPTION.

Appearance—The general appearance of the Bull Terrier is that of a symmetrical animal, an embodiment of agility, grace, elegance, and determination. *Head*—The head should be long, flat and wide between the ears, tapering to the nose, without cheek muscles. There should be a slight indentation down the face, without a "stop" between the eyes. The jaws should be long and very powerful, with a large black nose and open nostrils. Eyes small and very black, almond-shape preferred. The lips should meet as tightly as possible, without a fold. The teeth should be regular in shape, and should meet exactly; any deviation, such as "pig-jaw," or being "under-hung," is a great fault. *Ears*—Cropped dogs cannot win a prize at Shows held under Kennel Club Rules if born after 31st March, 1895. The ear to breed for, as settled by this Club, is a small semi-erect ear, but other ears do not disqualify. *Neck*—The neck should be long and slightly arched, nicely set into the shoulders, tapering to the head without any loose skin as found in the Bulldog. *Shoulders*—The shoulders should be strong, muscular, and slanting; the chest wide and deep, with ribs well rounded. *Back*—The back short and muscular, but not out of proportion to the general contour of the animal. *Legs*—The fore-legs should be perfectly straight, with well-developed muscles, not "out at shoulder," but set on the racing-lines, and very strong on the pastern-joints. The hind-legs are long, and, in proportion to the fore-legs, muscular, with good, strong, straight hocks, well let down near the ground. *Feet*—The feet more resemble those of a cat than a hare. *Colour*—Should be white. *Coat*—Short, close, and stiff to the touch, with a fine gloss. *Tail*—The tail should be short in proportion to the size of the dog, set on very low down, thick where it joins the body, and tapering to a fine point. It should be carried at an angle of about 45° without curl, and NEVER over the back. *Weight*—From 15 to 60 lbs.

With regard to *breeding*, the selection of the sire is, as in the case of all breeds, of the utmost importance. The use of dogs possessing the purest blood is the key-note to success. A dash of outside strain must, however, be resorted to occasionally to counter-act the evils of continued in-breeding, *e.g.*, deafness (which many *white* animals are subject to), want of vitality and rickets. Good specimens of doubtful or inferior ancestry have occasionally appeared on the show bench; but, when bred from, their progeny have been indifferent. On the other hand, many of our best dogs have sprung from parents who were indifferent specimens but whose *blood* was of the best. Hence, it is not the most perfect dog that sires the most perfect stock. Many breeders, especially beginners, have a tendency to run after the dog that is doing the most winning for the time being.

But this is not wise unless the *blood* is right; and it must be remembered that a dog which is constantly in demand will not, after a time, produce strong stock. When choosing the sire it should be noted whether he excels in those points wherein the bitch is lacking.

Bull Terriers are, as a rule, good mothers, fully recognising the nature and importance of their duties; and it is only in the case of a large litter that a foster has to be resorted to. The dam should not be permitted, however,

CH. WOODCOTE WONDER.

to bring up more than four or five puppies, as to bring up more involves too great a strain on her constitution. The puppies should be weaned in about six weeks' time; but they should be induced to lap after the third week, so that they may become accustomed to other food before the milk supply fails and the mother be relieved accordingly.

After weaning, the puppies must be closely watched; it is then that they commonly dwindle off. Teething is always a critical time, and a check at this period is always to be avoided, if possible, as it may greatly affect the future career.

At the earliest possible period the puppies should be allowed full liberty in the open air. They should never be kept housed-up or chained, for if in any way confined rickets is the invariable result; and as straight legs and good feet, together with well knit shoulders, are absolutely necessary for success on the show bench, rickets must be avoided at all costs. Phosphate of Lime is the most valuable preventive and may be given until the permanent teeth have made their appearance; it can be given in milk or with the solid food.

Ch. Charlwood Victor Wild.

The *food* at first should be light—such as puppy meal soaked with broth; a little later a small percentage of chopped meat may be added. When older, the food may be more varied. The evening meal should be of a soft nature; the morning meal should consist of such food as biscuits or hound meal. Bone meal added to the food will assist bone-development. Young puppies should be given at least four meals a day; after eight months, when the teeth wil

94

have been established, two meals will be found sufficient. Bones in their entirety should not be given as the act of gnawing tends to enlarge the cheek muscles and so prevents the head from having that clean wedge-shaped appearance desired by judges. The gnawing of wood, to which some dogs are greatly addicted, should also be prevented for the same reason.

WHITE WONDER.   SHERBOURNE QUEEN.

Bull Terriers can, with a little patience, be taught to do almost anything. They should be made accustomed to the lead when quite young and at this period should be taught to "show" themselves. To teach a dog to show to advantage, the lead should at first be attached to some stationary object and some dainty morsel of food, such as a piece of baked liver, should be shown and eventually given to him; in course of time, the mere raising of the hand will be sufficient to make him stand at attention and ready for the judge's inspection. As sporting dogs—though not classed as such—they readily take to the water and make splendid swimmers. They can be taught to retrieve and work hedgerows as well as many Spaniels or Retrievers. The writer has come 'across many which have a keen love for the gun and work excellently. As destroyers of vermin few breeds can equal them.

Ch. Woodcote Pride.

Although it may be considered strange, a dog of this breed will frequently form a close attachment to the feline species. Some of the older members of the fancy will probably remember that at a certain Birmingham Show one of the hampers, upon being opened, was found to contain a cat, curled up with the dog, to the amazement of all around; she was the dog's constant companion and had slipped in unawares! As a further instance of feline attachment, the case of the writer's own dog, Ben Caunt, may be mentioned. This dog formed a strange alliance with a black cat. They

96

were incessantly together; and whenever pussy went away from him he would howl until her return. Further, he would allow her to partake of his own food and would even stand aside until she had finished with it.

In the show ring, the dog must be put down as "gassy" and full of life as possible; hence he should be given daily exercise to develop the muscles and keep him in hard condition. The coat, being white, should be washed and

CH. DELPHINIUM WILD.

well groomed the day previous to the show. If his early education has been properly attended to he will show to great advantage in the ring and often score over a better dog whose education, in the matter of "showing," has been neglected until too late in life.

The coat being fine and stout in texture, enables the Bull Terrier to stand hot climates well; and being of a hardy nature, the dog can also stand the cold provided he be kept out of damp or draughty places.

The present type is considered by many to compare favourably with that of the past; but the writer is unable to take this view. Judging from the dogs which came under his notice at the last two shows at which he officiated (Streatham and the Kennel Club Show in October, 1906) the breed is, in his opinion, sadly deteriorating. The exhibits

Photo by W. Izon. Putney.]
SWEET LAVENDER.

presented two distinct types; the larger number were so weedy, high on leg, light of bone and snipey in muzzle as to resemble over-grown Whippets; many were as soft in expression as a Borzoi, the heads, though long, being entirely devoid of Bull Terrier expression and character. It is averred by some that the uncropped ear accounts for the soft expression, and to a certain extent this is true.

When breeding, the fancier would be well advised to keep in his mind's eye such dogs of the past as the following :—

Ch. Grand Prior ; Ch. Streatham ; Monarch II. ; Ch. Greenhill Romeo ; Ch. Woodcote Wonder (*see* page 362) ; Ch. Ambition ; Ch. Como ; Ch. Charlwood Victor Wild (*see* page 363) ; Sherbourne King ; White Sam ; White Wonder (*see* page 364) ; Ch. Greenhill Wonder ; Ch. Woodcote Wild ; Shifty Sarah ; Vitality ; Ch. Attraction ; Greenhill Maggie ; Greenhill Surprise ; White Queen ; and Hanover Daisy. It would not be fair to leave unmentioned such grand dogs, of an even date, as Ch. Mistress of the Robes and Max Marx. Gully the Great, Bendigo and Duke of Marlborough also made their mark as sires.

Amongst the best specimens of the breed to-day, mention may be made of Ch. Delphinium Wild and Sweet Lavender, the photos of which are here reproduced.

The pedigree of Woodcote Pride, one of the best " cropped " specimens, is as follows :

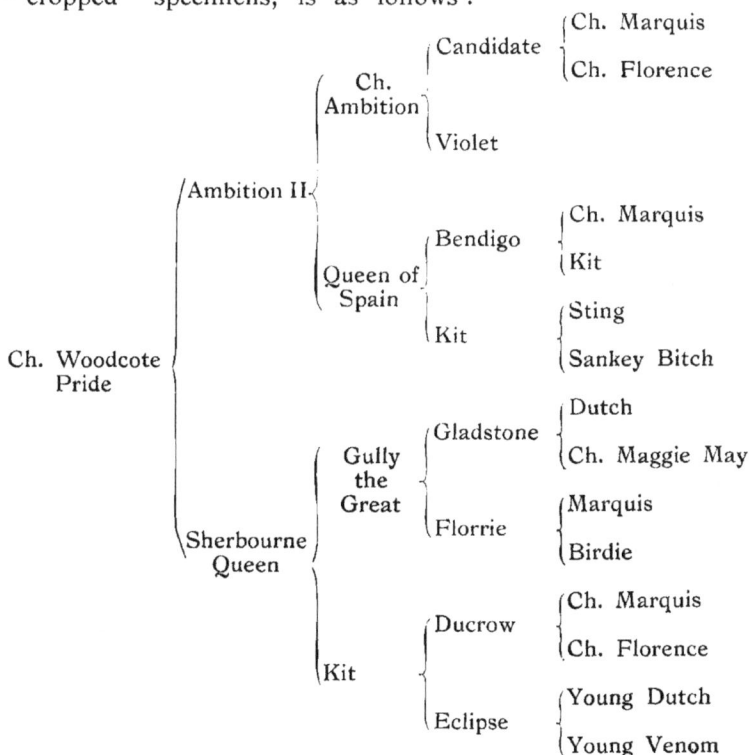

```
Ch. Woodcote Pride
├─ Ambition II
│   ├─ Ch. Ambition
│   │   ├─ Candidate
│   │   │   ├─ Ch. Marquis
│   │   │   └─ Ch. Florence
│   │   └─ Violet
│   └─ Queen of Spain
│       ├─ Bendigo
│       │   ├─ Ch. Marquis
│       │   └─ Kit
│       └─ Kit
│           ├─ Sting
│           └─ Sankey Bitch
└─ Sherbourne Queen
    ├─ Gully the Great
    │   ├─ Gladstone
    │   │   ├─ Dutch
    │   │   └─ Ch. Maggie May
    │   └─ Florrie
    │       ├─ Marquis
    │       └─ Birdie
    └─ Kit
        ├─ Ducrow
        │   ├─ Ch. Marquis
        │   └─ Ch. Florence
        └─ Eclipse
            ├─ Young Dutch
            └─ Young Venom
```

It is very regretful that we have altogether lost the grand little ones of from 16 to 18 lbs. weight; dogs such as Ch. Florence, the dam of Candidate and Ducrow.

Some of the past celebrities retained their clean, chiselled heads for a great number of years—in fact, they were as clean in head and devoid of a suspicion of cheek bump when their roll was called as our eight months' puppies of to-day. The causes of the degeneration in the breed are varied; many of our best sires and brood bitches have been exported to America, and the abolition of cropping has no doubt caused a large number of the old exhibitors to give up the breed.

Of the clubs promoted in the interests of the breed may be mentioned the Bull Terrier Club, the Northern Bull Terrier Club, the British Bull Terrier Club, and the Scottish Bull Terrier Club.

W. J. PEGG.

Editorial Note.—Mr. W. J. Pegg, the writer of the above article, has spoken of the Bull Terrier as being well adapted to the climate of India, and has also spoken of the breed as being useful in different kinds of sport. The late Mr. C. W. A. Bruce, of the Indian Forest Department, narrated these stories in the *Forester.* "Alice" was a pure Bull Terrier bred from imported parents. At the end of the cold season in 1898, Mr. Bruce, after a long day's work at forest surveying, was returning to camp when he came upon the track of a bull bison, and thinking there would still be time, with luck, to come up to him before dark, his sporting instincts were aroused, and, accompanied by his hunter, a coolie, and his terrier Alice, he started in pursuit. Just as he arrived at the edge of the bush, to which he had tracked the bison, his hunter pointed to the track of an elephant, whispering "to-day." Mr. Bruce replied that at present he was after bison and was not going to tackle elephants with a 12-bore paradox. However, he had only

100

gone about 100 yards very cautiously, when he was startled by a ponderous sigh, and peering through the undergrowth he saw the hind-quarters of an elephant about six yards off. The huge beast was nonchalantly pouring dust on his back, and it was this sound that had attracted Mr. Bruce's attention. The chance was too good to be missed. He

Mr. Bruce's Bull Terriers, Sam and Toy, in Camp, in Upper Burma.

signalled to the hunter and together they crept back to the coolie with the dog, and told the former what was ahead, and that he was to wait with the dog, and on no account to let her go. Then creeping back to where he had seen the elephant, but wishing to find a more vulnerable looking spot than the root of his tail, he started crawling round to his side. Mr. Bruce had just got a view of a beautiful, gleaming pair of white tusks, when he heard a pattering in the leaves behind him. Looking round he saw his dog Alice, her eyes blazing with excitement, and her hair erect. She could see that her master was after something and wished to have a bite in. In vain Mr. Bruce made a grab at her as she went past, but says the narrator—"the rest baffles description. I heard a tempest of barks, terrified and prolonged trumpeting, combined with a noise as if a steam-mowing machine was at work. I thought that directly the terrier found her antagonist was a stone or two above her fighting weight she would run back home, and I anticipated her running between my legs, with the enraged tusker in full cry, running tusks down, and the picture 'pleased me not.'' Mr. Bruce and his hunter hurriedly climbed a tree, and were there spectators of a most exciting scene. The elephant was seen terrified and prancing round like a top, and trumpeting for all he was worth, the terrier making ferocious rushes to try and get a grip. The tusker would then charge, and, as the dog retreated, dig ferociously at her with his right tusk, the dog, of course, being by that time some yards further off. Mr. Bruce here thought it time to intervene, and he fired his gun into the elephant's head. This started him off like a run-away locomotive, and the terrier, shrieking with delight, went after him. The dog headed the beast and went snapping alongside. Mr. Bruce then again fired his "brown-bess" and the elephant swerved away to the left, not to return. Mr. Bruce climbed down and, after an interval of about five minutes, the terrier turned up, tongue out, fearfully pleased with herself. She had utterly defeated the King of the Forest, routing him trunk and tusks. Her owner then returned to the coolie. He explained that he had got frightened, climbed a tree, and let the dog go. After sorrowfully kicking the coolie "the three men and a dog" returned to camp.

Another exploit of this game little dog was the following:—

One hot day in April, on arriving at a small village, Mr. Bruce and an assistant were met by two natives, who had previously been his companions in many a weary tramp, and who informed him that a herd of bison were in the habit of coming from the neighbouring woods every day, morning and evening, to eat the tender grass shoots in the " Indaing."

Mr. C. Bruce's SAM and YOUNG SAM.
YOUNG SAM (in the foreground) is a son of SAM and TOY, and was bred in Burma.

The assistant, whose first year out had not come to an end, was anxious for a try at something, so they arranged to set out the next morning accompanied by the natives, and, of course, Alice, to look out for tracks round the wood. Tracks all round were very plentiful, in fact, too much so, and it was nigh to impossible to distinguish the fresher ones from those a few days old. The sun eventually got too much for the hunters, and they camped under a bank near a fetid pool, into which the Bull Terrier wallowed and lay gasping. After many weary hours of waiting, the watchers were rewarded by the noise occasioned by the approaching bison, and peering over a small Kuin (an area devoid of trees) saw grazing on the new shoots of elephant grass a herd of thirteen bison. Whispering to the men to hold on to the dog until they heard a shot, Mr. Bruce crawled on his hands and knees until in a position to fire. He then took a careful plug at the shoulder, and then the change! Every animal threw up its head and made for the jungle. Tearing across an open strip diagonally to cut them off, Mr. Bruce was able to get in a beautiful shot at one of the bison, which dropped stone dead. Thoughtlessly running on in the broad track left by this flying herd, he was suddenly brought up on hearing a deep snort, and, looking forward, discerned in the gloom the head of a bison thrown well up, and staring wild-eyed at him. Downhill dashed the infuriated brute. Mr. Bruce wisely determining to reserve his shot till the last moment, then, letting off both barrels, he sprang aside. At this juncture his foot unfortunately caught in a creeper, and he fell headlong, his gun at the same time flying from his hand. An instant, and he felt his coat torn open and himself lying down with the bison's chest on his outstretched thigh. Immediately he saw a flash of white, and his Bull Terrier had leapt across her master's body, and closed with the bison, fixing her teeth firmly into the great beast's india-rubber-like nose. The bison struggled to its feet, and Mr. Bruce did not take long to follow its example, his only idea being to get away; feeling very shaken, the sportsman blundered along through the jungle till he suddenly felt himself falling, and he found himself full length in a deep narrow nullah. Going down this for about fifty yards, he reached a pool, fetid and stinking, yet containing liquid, perhaps 50% of water anyway. He drank until, feeling revived, he got out of the nullah, and made his way back to his men. Shortly after Alice turned up, wagging her tail, and, except that she was very blown, appearing none the worse for her encounter with the bison.

These stories are narrrated to show that the Bull Terrier will thrive very well in a hot climate and can be trained to make an excellent sporting dog. Mr. Bruce had other Bull Terriers in Burma (*see* the photos on pages 370 and 372) some of which he bred there. He trained one or two of these dogs to keep to heel, and when he was stalking big game

Photo by R. B. Cosway, London.]
Lady Evelyn Ewart's TWINKLE LITTLE STAR.

the dogs would creep noiselessly behind and carefully avoid treading on any stick or leaf which might arouse the quarry. Mr. Bruce was one of the most celebrated shikaris and wrote several chapters in Rowland Ward's book *The Great and Small Game of India.*

It may be added that Alice came of good English stock, her grand-sire being Mr. W. J. Pegg's White Wonder (*see* page 364).

GEN. ED.

105

Miniature or Toy Bull Terriers, which should scale under 10 lbs. are a miniature edition of the larger breed ; their points are exactly the same as those of the larger variety (*see* page 360, *supra*).

Unfortunately, great difficulty is experienced in breeding the Toy variety with the small "slit" eye ; most of the dogs have prominent or "goggle" eyes ; and Toys, generally, lack the finish and filled-up muzzle of their larger brethren.

The best specimen of to-day is, unmistakably, Lady Evelyn Ewart's fascinating little specimen Twinkle Little Star, a photo of which is here re-produced (*see* page 374).

Now that the variety has a Club to foster its interests there is every likelihood of these little dogs becoming more popular and more frequently shown.

W. J. PEGG.

THE BULL-TERRIER.

" Nor was he of the thievish sort,
Or one whom blood allures,
But innocent was all his sport
Whom you have torn for yours.

My dog! what remedy remains,
Since, teach you all I can,
I see you, after all my pains,
So much resemble man ?"

—COWPER.

THE Bull-terrier is now a gentlemanly and respectably owned dog, wearing an immaculate white coat and a burnished silver collar; he has dealings with aristocracy, and is no longer contemned for keeping bad company. But a generation or two ago he was commonly the associate of rogues and vagabonds, skulking at the heels of such members of society as Mr. William Sikes, whom he accompanied at night on darksome business to keep watch outside while Bill was within, cracking the crib. The burglar and the bruiser usually kept one or more of such dogs, and the companionship was appropriate. Landseer took the Bull-terrier as the typical representative of low life, as the antithesis of the patrician Deerhound, and painted him with bleared eye and swollen lips and a blackguardly scowl that repelled familiarity. In those days the dog's ears were closely cropped, not for the sake of embellishment, but as a measure of protection against the fangs of his opponent in the pit when money was laid upon the result of a well-fought fight to the death. For fighting was the acknowledged vocation of his order, and he was bred and trained to the work. He knew something of rats, too, and many of his kind were famed in the land for their prowess in this direction. Jimmy Shaw's Jacko could finish off sixty rats in three minutes, and on one occasion made a record by killing a thousand in a trifle over an hour and a half.

At one period in England, Bull-terriers were used in gladiatorial contests, being pitted against so formidable an antagonist as the lion, as they were at Warwick in 1825. They were then heavier and more powerful dogs than are their artistically bred descendants. Fifty-five pounds was not an uncommon weight. One might

MR. S. E. SHIRLEY'S NELSON (1872).

almost suppose that they had an infusion of Mastiff blood in their veins. Their colour, too, was not necessarily white. Brindle and fawn frequently occurred, and many were black and tan; but the larger number, next to pure brindle, were white with fallow markings, similar in distribution to the colours seen at the present day in the Boston Terrier, who is a near relative.

The breed is sufficiently modern to leave no doubt as to its derivation. In the first quarter of the nineteenth century attention was being directed to the improvement of terriers generally, and new types were sought for. They were alert, agile little dogs, excellent for work in the country; but the extravagant Corinthians of the time—the young gamesters who patronised the prize-ring and the cock-pit—desired to have a dog who should do something more than kill rats, or unearth the fox, or bolt the otter : which accomplishments afforded no amusement to the Town. They wanted a dog combining all the dash and gameness of the terrier with the heart and courage and fighting instinct of the Bulldog. Wherefore the terrier and the Bulldog were crossed.

CH. BLOOMSBURY YOUNG KING
BY BLOOMSBURY KING—BLOOMSBURY NORAH.
BRED AND OWNED BY MR. J. HAYNES.

A large type of terrier was chosen, and this would be the smooth-coated black-and-tan, or the early English white terrier ; but probably both were used indifferently, and for a considerable period. The result gave the young bucks what they required : a dog that was at once a determined vermin killer and an intrepid fighter, upon whose skill in the pit wagers might with confidence be laid.

The animal, however, was neither a true terrier nor a true Bulldog, but an uncompromising mongrel ; albeit he served his immediate purpose, and was highly valued for his pertinacity, if not for his appearance. In 1806 Lord Camelford possessed one for which he had paid the very high price of eighty-four guineas, and which he presented to Belcher, the pugilist. This dog was figured in *The Sporting Magazine* of the time. He was a short-legged, thick-set fawn-coloured specimen, with closely amputated ears, a broad blunt muzzle, and a considerable lay-back ; and this was the kind of dog which continued for many years to be known as the Bull-and-terrier. He was essentially a man's dog, and was vastly in favour among the undergraduates of Oxford and Cambridge.

Gradually the Bulldog element, at first so pronounced, was reduced to something like a fourth degree, and, with the terrier character predominating, the head was sharpened, the limbs were lengthened and straightened until little remained of the Bulldog strain but the dauntless heart and the fearless fighting spirit, together with the frequent reversion to brindle colouring, which was the last outward and visible characteristic to disappear

Within the remembrance of men not yet old the Bull-terrier was as much marked with fawn, brindle, or even black, as are the Fox-terriers of our own period. Bill Sikes' companion, who came to so undignified an end, was a bandy-legged, coarse, and heavy creature with a black patch on his eye and one or two patches on his body. But fifty years or so ago white was becoming frequent, and was much admired. A strain of pure white was bred by James Hinks, a well-known dog-dealer of Birmingham, and it is no doubt to Hinks that we are indebted for the elegant Bull-terrier of the type that we know to-day. These Birmingham dogs showed a refinement and grace and an absence of the crook-legs and coloured patches which betrayed that Hinks had been using an out-cross with the Egnlish white terrier, thus getting away further still from the Bulldog. Many persons objected that with the introduction of new blood he had eliminated the pugnacity which had been one of the most valued attributes of the breed. But the charge was not justified, and to prove that his strain had lost none of the cherished quality of belligerence Hinks backed his bitch Puss against one of the old bull-faced type for a five-pound note and a case of champagne.

BULL-TERRIER, MILLSTONE HERO.

BULL-TERRIER BITCH, MILLSTONE VENUS.

The fight took place at Tupper's in Long Acre, and in half an hour Puss had killed her opponent, her own injuries being so slight that she was able to appear the next morning at a dog show and take a prize for her good looks and condition.

Madman was another of Hinks's terriers, and the names of this pair were so persistently adopted by other owners for other dogs that it is impossible now to trace a pedigree back to the genuine originals. In the Kennel Club Stud Book for 1874 there are a dozen Bull-terriers all named Madman.

With the advent of the Hinks strain in 1862 the short-faced dog fell into disrepute, and pure white became the accepted colour. There was a wide latitude in the matter of weight. If all other points were good, a dog might weigh anything between 10 and 38 lb., but classes were usually divided for those above and those below 16 lb. The type became fixed, and it was ruled that the perfect Bull-terrier " must have a long head, wide between the ears, level jaws, a small black eye, a large black nose, a long neck, straight forelegs, a small hare foot, a narrow chest, deep brisket, powerful loin, long body, a tail set and carried low, a fine coat, and small ears well hung and dropping forward."

Idstone, who wrote this description in 1872, earnestly insisted that the ears of all dogs should be left uncut and as Nature made them ; but for twenty years thereafter the ears of the Bull-terrier continued to be cropped to a thin, erect point. The practice of cropping, it is true, was even then illegal and punishable by law, but, although there were occasional convictions under the Cruelty to Animals Act, the dog owners who admired the alertness and perkiness of the cut ear ignored the risk they ran, and it was not until the Kennel Club took resolute action against the practice that cropping was entirely abandoned.

The prompting cause of this decision was a prosecution at Worship Street police court early in 1895 against three offenders " for causing to be tortured and for actually torturing and ill-treating, by cutting its ears, a certain dog." The dog in question is believed to have been an Irish terrier, but whatever its breed the three defendants were each fined £5 and £2 2s. costs. The case was discussed at a meeting of the Kennel Club, and, although the members were not at first in full agreement, yet it was ultimately decided and a rule was formulated that " no dog born after the 31st of March, 1895, should, if cropped, win a prize at any show held under Kennel Club rules."

The president of the Kennel Club, Mr. S. E. Shirley, M.P., had himself been a prominent owner and breeder of the Bull-terrier. His Nelson, bred by Joe Willock, was celebrated as an excellent example of the small-sized terrier, at a time, however, when there were not a great many competitors of the highest quality. His Dick, also, was a remarkably good dog. Earlier specimens which have left their names in the history of the breed were Hinks's Old Dutch, who was, perhaps, even a more perfect terrier than the same breeder's Madman and Puss ; Alfred George's Spring, G. Smith's Young Puss, Tredennick's Bertie, and R. J. Hartley's Magnet and Violet, who are said to have been a magnificent pair. Godfree's Young Victor, although disfigured by a patch over his eye, was famous for his perfection of shape and his success as a sire, and many of our recent champions have his name in their pedigrees. Sir W. E. H. Verney's Ch. Tarquin, a son of Young Victor, was the most distinguished Bull-terrier during the four years prior to 1878. He was a pure white dog, weighing 45 lb. His recorded measurements may be useful for the purpose of comparison with those of the terriers of the present day. They are : Nose to stop, 3¾ inches ; stop to occiput, 5¼ inches ; length from occiput to root of tail, 30¾ inches ; girth of skull, 18 inches ; girth of muzzle, 12¼ inches ; girth of chest, 26¼ inches ; girth of loins, 22 inches ; girth of forearm, 6¾ inches ; girth of pastern, 4 inches ; hock to ground, 5 inches ; height at shoulder, 18½ inches.

Lancashire and Yorkshire have always been noted for good Bull-terriers, and the best of the breed have usually been produced in the neighbourhoods of Leeds, Bradford, Manchester, Bolton, Liverpool, and Birmingham. At one time Londoners gave careful attention to the breed, stimulated thereto by the encouragement of Mr. Shirley and the success of Alfred George.

Of recent years the Bull-terrier has not been a great favourite, and it has sadly deteriorated in type; but there are signs that the variety is again coming into repute,

and within the past twelve months many admirable specimens—as nearly perfect, perhaps, as many that won honour in former generations—have been brought into prominence. Among dogs, for example, there are Mr. E. T. Pimm's Sweet Lavender, Dr. M. Amsler's MacGregor, Mr. Chris Houlker's His Highness, Mr. A. Haustein's Emporium King, and Mr. J. Haynes' Bloomsbury Young King. Among bitches there are Mrs. Kipping's Delphinium Wild and Desdemona, Mr. Hornby's Lady Sweetheart, Mr. W. Mayor's Mill Girl, Mr. T. Gannaway's Charlwood Belle, Dr. J. W. Low's Bess of Hardwicke, and Mrs. E. G. Money's Eastbourne Tarqueenia. While these and such as these beautiful and typical terriers are being bred and exhibited there is no cause to fear a further decline in popularity for a variety so eminently engaging.

It is satisfactory to note that more atten-tion is now being paid to the type of ears of the Bull-terrier. The ear best suited for cropping was not the ear which in its natural condition was most to be admired. Consequently, it has taken a long time to breed out the wrong form; but even yet there is no definite standard fixed for the ear of the Bull-terrier, and one may see them of any shape, from the "tulip" to the "button," from the "drop" to the "rose." The ear carriage is so important a point in the appearance of a terrier that it is high time that a definite form should be agreed upon as the standard of perfection. The club description is not altogether satisfying, and it might well be improved by careful revision. As it is at present it is as follows :

1. **General Appearance.**—The general appearance of the Bull-terrier is that of a symmetrical animal, the embodiment of agility, grace, elegance, and determination.

2. **Head.**—The head should be long, flat, and wide between the ears, tapering to the nose, without cheek muscles. There should be a slight indentation down the face, without a stop between the eyes. The jaws should be long and very powerful, with a large black nose and open nostrils. Eyes small and very black, almond shape preferred. The lips should meet as tightly as possible, without a fold. The teeth should be regular and large, and should meet exactly ; any deviation, such as pig-jaw, or being under-hung, is a great fault.

3. **Ears.**—The ears, when cropped, should be done scientifically and according to fashion. Cropped dogs cannot win a prize at shows held under Kennel Club rules, if born after March 31st, 1895. When not cropped, it should be a semi-erect ear, but others do not disqualify.

4. **Neck.**—The neck should be long and slightly arched, nicely set into the shoulders, tapering to the head without any loose skin, as found in the Bulldog.

5. **Shoulders.**—The shoulders should be strong, muscular, and slanting ; the chest wide and deep, with ribs well rounded.

6. **Back.**—The back short and muscular, but not out of proportion to the general contour of the animal.

7. **Legs.**—The forelegs should be perfectly straight, with well-developed muscles ; not out at shoulder, but set on the racing lines, and very strong at the pastern joints. The hind legs are long and, in proportion to the forelegs, muscular, with good strong, straight hocks, well let down near the ground.

8. Feet.—The feet more resemble those of a cat than a hare.

9. Colour.—Should be white.

10. Coat.—Short, close, and stiff to the touch, with a fine gloss.

11. Tail.—Short in proportion to the size of the dog, set on very low down, thick where it joins the body, and tapering to a fine point. It should be carried at an angle of about 45 degrees, without curl, and *never* over the back.

12. Height at Shoulders.—From 12 to 18 inches.

13. Weight.—From 15 lbs. to 50 lbs.

Scale of Points.

Head	20
Eyes	15
Ears	15
Neck and body	20
Legs and feet	15
Coat and tail	15
Total . . .	100

Two influences contributed to what one may hope was only a temporary lull in the favour which this terrier formerly enjoyed:—the rule against cropping, which was deemed to have robbed the dog of one of its chief charms; and the circumstance that when that rule was passed a large number of our best Bull-terriers were forthwith exported to purchasers in other countries where cropping remains fashionable. Many went to Holland, many to Germany, some to France, but most of all to the United States.

The Bull-terrier is one of the breeds in which America holds a strong hand, and it is a fact that more good specimens can be exhibited at a New York show than are benched throughout the whole of England in the entire year. From their British-bred terriers, such as Grand Duke, Gully the Great, Carney, and Cordona, and many more recent importations, the Americans are steadily multiplying their stock. With them it is a principle to breed abundantly, so that they may have more from which to select their potential champions. Perhaps they are disposed to favour longer bodies and shorter legs than we care for; but, as a rule, their Bull-terriers are kept similar in type to ours, and many an English breeder might envy them the possession of such terriers as Starlight and Diamond King, Dusty Miller, Young Marquis, and Edgewood Fancy; while their great champions, Princeton Monarch, Edgewood Crystal, Ajax of the Point, and Faultless of the Point, are superlative specimens of the race such as are no longer to be equalled on this side of the Atlantic.   R. L.

DR. MAURICE AMSLER'S BULL-TERRIERS AT WORK.

Photograph by Dr. Maurice Amsler, Eton.

Bull-Terrier of the famous Bloomsbury strain.

THE BULL-TERRIER

THE Bull-terrier is now a gentlemanly and respectably owned dog, wearing an immaculate white coat and a burnished silver collar ; he has dealings with aristocracy, and is no longer contemned for keeping bad company. But a generation or two ago he was commonly the associate of rogues and vaga-bonds, skulking at the heels of such members of society as Mr. William Sikes, whom he accompanied at night on darksome business to keep watch outside while Bill was within, crack-ing the crib. In those days the dog's ears were closely cropped, not for the sake of embellishment, but as a measure of protection against the fangs of his opponent in the pit when money was laid upon the result of a well-fought fight to the death. For fighting was the acknowledged vocation of his order, and he was bred and trained to the work. He knew something of rats, too, and many of his kind were famed in the land for their prowess in this direction. Jimmy Shaw's Jacko could finish off sixty rats in three minutes, and on one occasion made a record by killing a thousand in a trifle over an hour and a half.

The breed is sufficiently modern to leave no doubt as to its derivation. In the first quarter of the nineteenth century attention was being directed to the improvement of terriers generally, and new types were sought for. They were alert, agile little dogs, excellent for work in the country ; but the extravagant Corinthians of the time—the young gamesters who patronised the prize-ring and the cock-pit—desired to have a dog who should do something more than kill rats, or unearth the fox, or bolt the otter : which accomplishments afforded no amusement to the Town. They wanted a dog combining all the dash and gameness of the terrier with the heart and courage and fighting instinct of the Bulldog. Wherefore the terrier and the Bulldog were crossed. A large type of terrier was chosen, and this would be the smooth-coated Black and Tan, or the early English White Terrier ; but probably both were used indifferently, and for a considerable period. The result gave the young bucks what they required : a dog that was at once a determined vermin killer and an intrepid fighter, upon whose skill in the pit wagers might with confidence be laid.

The animal, however, was neither a true terrier nor a true Bulldog, but an uncompromising mongrel ; albeit he served his immediate purpose, and was highly valued for his pertinacity, if not for his appearance. In 1806 Lord Camelford possessed one for which he had paid the very high price of eighty-four guineas, and which he presented to Belcher, the pugilist. This dog was figured in *The Sporting Magazine* of the time. He was a short-legged, thick-set, fawn-coloured specimen, with closely amputated ears, a broad blunt muzzle, and a considerable lay-back ; and this was the kind of dog which continued for many years to be known as the Bull-and-terrier. He was essentially a man's dog, and was vastly in favour among the undergraduates of Oxford and Cambridge.

Gradually the Bulldog element, at first pronounced, was reduced to something like a fourth degree, and, with the terrier character predominating, the head was sharpened, the limbs were lengthened and straightened until little remained of the Bulldog strain but the dauntless heart and the fearless fighting spirit, together with the frequent reversion to brindle colouring, which was the last outward and visible characteristic to disappear.

Within the remembrance of men not yet old the Bull-terrier was as much marked with fawn, brindle, or even black, as are the Fox-terriers of our own period. But fifty years or so ago white was becoming frequent, and was much admired. A strain of pure white was bred by James Hinks, a well-known dog-dealer of Birmingham, and it is no doubt to Hinks that we are indebted for the elegant Bull-terrier of the type that we know to-day. These Birmingham dogs showed a refinement and grace and an absence of the crook-legs and coloured patches which betrayed that Hinks had been using an outcross with the English White Terrier, thus getting away further still from the Bulldog.

With the advent of the Hinks strain in 1862 the short-faced dog fell into disrepute, and pure white became the accepted colour. There was a wide latitude in the matter of weight. If all other points were good, a dog might weigh anything between 10 and 38 lbs., but classes were usually divided for those above and those below 16 lb. The type became fixed, and it was ruled that the perfect Bull-terrier " must have a long head, wide between the ears, level jaws, a small black eye, a large black nose, a long neck, straight fore-legs, a small hare foot, a narrow chest, deep brisket, powerful loin, long body, a tail set and carried low, a fine coat, and small ears well hung and dropping forward."

Idstone, who wrote this description in 1872, earnestly insisted that the ears of all dogs should be left uncut and as Nature made them ; but for twenty years thereafter the ears of the Bull-terrier continued to be cropped to a thin, erect point. The practice of cropping, it is true, was even then illegal and punishable by law, but, although there were occasional convictions under the Cruelty to Animals Act, the dog owners who admired the alertness and perkiness of the cut ear ignored the risk they ran, and it was not until the Kennel Club took resolute action against the practice that cropping was entirely abandoned.

The president of the Kennel Club, Mr. S. E. Shirley, M.P., had himself been a prominent owner and breeder of the Bull-terrier. His Nelson, bred by Joe Willock, was celebrated as an excellent example of the small-sized terrier, at a time,

117

however, when there were not a great many competitors of the highest quality. His Dick, also, was a remarkably good dog. Earlier specimens which have left their names in the history of the breed were Hinks's Old Dutch, who was, perhaps, even a more perfect terrier than the same breeder's Madman and Puss.

Lancashire and Yorkshire have always been noted for good Bull-terriers, and the best of the breed have usually been produced in the neighbourhoods of Leeds, Bradford, Manchester, Bolton, and Liverpool, while Birmingham also shared in the reputation. At one time Londoners gave careful attention to the breed, stimulated thereto by the encouragement of Mr. Shirley and the success of Alfred George.

Of recent years the Bull-terrier has not been a great favourite, and it has sadly deteriorated in type ; but there are signs that the variety is again coming into repute, and within the past two years many admirable specimens—as nearly perfect, perhaps, as many that won honour in former generations— have been brought into prominence. Among dogs, for example, there are Mr. E. T. Pimm's Sweet Lavender, Dr. M. Amsler's MacGregor, Mr. Chris Houlker's His Highness, and Mr. J. Haynes' Bloomsbury Young King. Among bitches there are Mrs. Kipping's Delphinium Wild and Desdemona, Mr. Hornby's Lady Sweetheart, Mr. W. Mayor's Mill Girl, Mr. T. Gannaway's Charlwood Belle, Dr. J. W. Low's Bess of Hardwicke, and Mrs. E. G. Money's Eastbourne Tarqueenia. While these and such as these beautiful and typical terriers are being bred and exhibited there is no cause to fear a further decline in popularity for a variety so eminently engaging.

The club description is as follows :—

General Appearance—The general appearance of the Bull-terrier is that of a symmetrical animal, the embodiment of agility, grace, elegance, and determination. **Head**—The head should be long, flat, and wide between the ears, tapering to the nose, without cheek muscles. There should be a slight indentation down the face, without a stop between the eyes. The jaws should be long and very powerful, with a large black nose and open nostrils. Eyes small and very black, almond hape preferred. The lips should meet as tightly as possible, without

118

a fold. The teeth should be regular in shape, and should meet exactly ; any deviation, such as pigjaw, or being underhung, is a great fault. **Ears**—The ears, when cropped, should be done scientifically and according to fashion. Cropped dogs cannot win a prize at shows held under Kennel Club rules, if born after March 31st, 1895. When not cropped, it should be a semi-erect ear, but others do not disqualify. **Neck**—The neck should be long and slightly arched, nicely set into the shoulders tapering to the head without any loose skin, as found in the Bulldog. **Shoulders**—The shoulders should be strong, muscular, and slanting ; the chest wide and deep, with ribs well rounded. **Back**—The back short and muscular, but not out of proportion to the general contour of the animal. **Legs**—The fore-legs should be perfectly straight, with well-developed muscles ; not out at shoulder, but set on the racing lines, and very strong at the pastern joints. The hind-legs are long and, in proportion to the fore-legs, muscular, with good strong, straight hocks, well let down near the ground. **Feet**—The feet more resemble those of a cat than a hare. **Colour**—Should be white. **Coat**—Short, close, and stiff to the touch, with a fine gloss. **Tail**—Short in proportion to the size of the dog, set on very low down, thick where it joins the body, and tapering to a fine point. It should be carried at an angle of about 45 degrees, without curl, and never over the back. **Height at Shoulders**—From 12 to 18 inches. **Weight**—From 15 lb. to 50 lb.

124

WOODCOTE WONDER.

This famous dog was whelped in England and was about five years old when brought to America. His weight was 51½ pounds, and height 20½ inches. He defeated nearly everything shown against him for nearly ten years, both in England and America, and won enough championships to crown half a dozen dogs champion. His stud fee was $100, and we print his picture as an illustration of a perfect type of the bench show Bull Terrier, although of late years some of the faddists have been breeding a dog lighter in build and higher on his legs.

CHAMPION VIRGINALIS.

This bitch, whose picture will surely attract your attention, died in the summer of 1914. She was owned by Gilt Edge Kennels and was the most typical Bull Terrier bitch, of the bench-show type, in America. These illustrations are published for comparisons between the bench-show type and the pit-dog type. You will notice that many of the latter would make typical show specimens as far as conformation is concerned; but the trouble is that the pit dog fancier is not breeding to standard nor for beauty. For that reason an organization with an accepted, recognized standard is needed for the breed.

THE GAS-HOUSE DOG.

One of the most famous and widely quoted dogs as the foundation stock of Pit-Bull Terriers in America was The Gas-House Dog. The Gas-House Dog, or to speak more properly, McDonald's Grip, was a brindle dog with white blaze in face, white ring about neck, white breast and paws. He was the property of the late John McDonald, who at the time of ownership had charge of the gas-house stables in Boston, and who died in 1909. Grip was bred in Boston and was always owned there. He was whelped in the early seventies, dying about 1882. The Gas-House Dog was considered to have no superior in his class at 31 pounds. His most noted battle was with the no less celebrated Blind Dog, which ended in a draw, free fight and wrangle after the dogs had gone nearly three hours. The Blind Dog had previously beaten Burke's Spring,

another dog in the kennel, resulting in the ruina-
tion of both dogs and a serious financial loss to his
owner. A lead or chain securely fastened to a harness, the other end of the chain snapped in a ring
which runs on a strong wire stretched across the
yard about six feet above the ground, will not only
safely hold your dog, but will give him an opportunity to get some necessary exercise. Your dogs
should not be fought until fully matured, say
eighteen months old.

JACK SUTTON.

Jack Sutton, A.
K. C. 66348, is a
specimen of the
Irish Pit Bull Ter-
rier. He is out of
Sutton's Molly and
these dogs in Ire-
land are classified
as the Murphy
strain. They are
acknowledged as
good pit dogs. This
dog was for some
time at the head of
F. L. Dunable's
Kennels of Clay
Center, Kans., but has been used for stud purposes
only lately, and is at this writing at the kennels of
Harvey Peace in Mississippi.

Now, if you have followed these instructions carefully and intelligently, you should have your dog in as good a condition as it is possible for human skill to make him.

If you cannot give the time to train your own dog, by all means know the man you hire, and be sure he is above being bribed.

KING PADDY.

King Paddy was bred and owned by L. A. Swineford of Ashland, Ohio. He was whelped April 16, 1909; weight on chain, 40 pounds; brindle in color. He is of the family of Delihant's Paddy, and won first prize at the 'Cleveland (Ohio) Fanciers' Club Show in 1913. The Pit Bull Terriers had no class, consequently he, together with his son Kelley and his half-sister Queen, all competed with English Bull Terriers. They each came out of the judging ring with a blue ribbon (first prize). Mr. Swineford says of Paddy: "King Paddy is

Champion Virginalis

Colby's Pincher

Colby's Tige

fawn Bull Terriers as well as whites, brindle being a color that is always associated with hardihood, and which is certainly handsome. The dog still retains his pugilistic propensities, which are bred in him and inherent to his nature. He is the game-cock of the canine species, and undoubtedly the finest exponent of the 'noble art' as applied to dogs, which puritans would probably describe as the 'ignoble' art."

The Kennel Bosses

Compliments of the Burnett Kennels Co.,
Knoxville, Tenn.

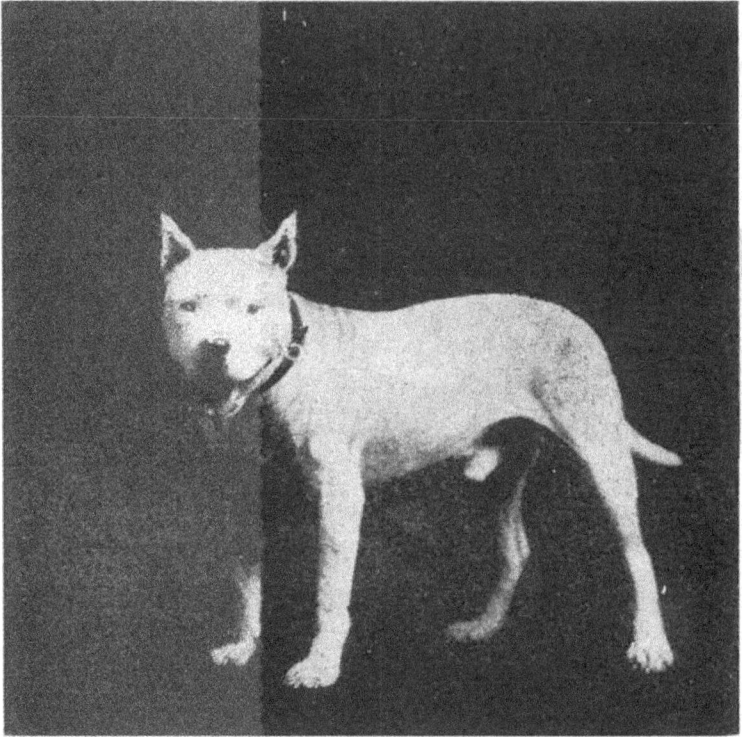

W. S. Semmes and Big Jack

TIGER JIM

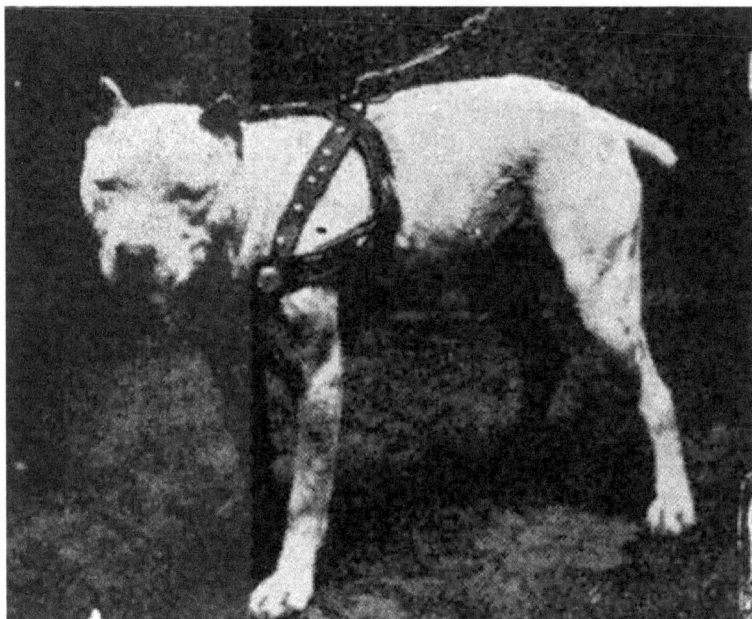

Champion Dan

Champion Pilot

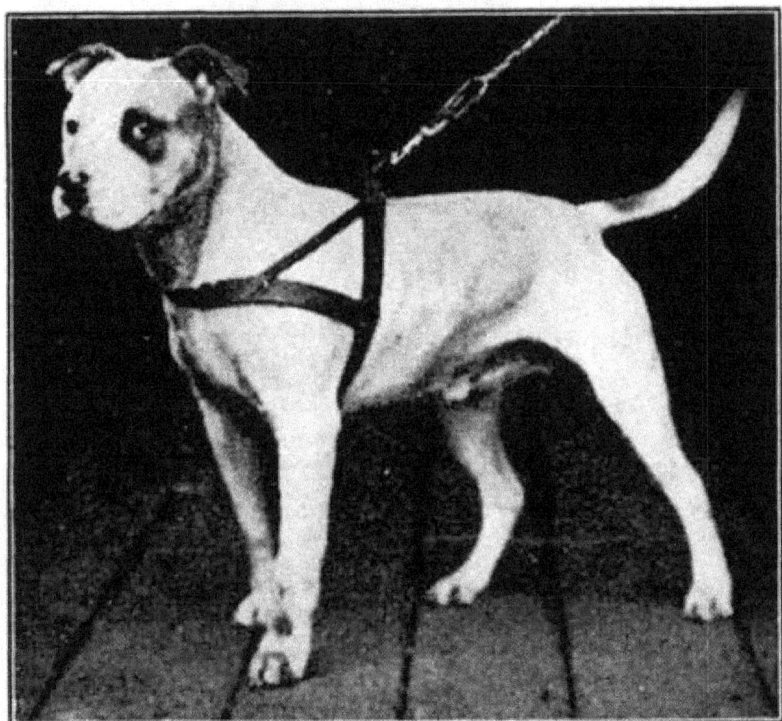

Redican's Major

BULL TERRIER

BULL TERRIER

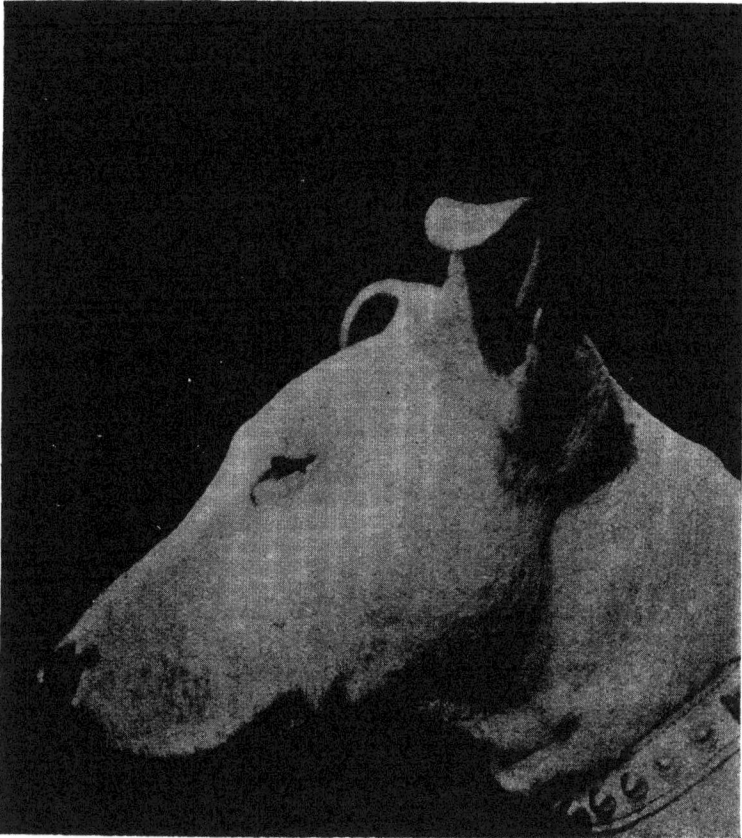

HEAD OF A BULL TERRIER

143

A BULL-TERRIER CH. YOUNG CAVALIER . . . no
rum or queer kiddy or man of cash from Tothil Street
in the West to N.E. Holloway, far less any swell rising
sixteen . . . . must have a take of the new cut at the heels
of himself . . . .' (Egan, describing the Bull-Terrier).

THE BULL-TERRIER

Origin, Terrier and Bulldog cross ; size, strength, **vitality** was needed ; a fighting dog.

A man ; his Bull-terrier on a walk ; the local butcher's lurcher ; they met. The Bull-terrier cried for help ; much excitement; the butcher delighted because the lurcher won.

Next day the same thing happened (more or less) ; the lurcher won easily ; the Bull-terrier had lost his heart.

Third day the butcher's friends collected. They met ; the lurcher madly and manfully fought to win, fought to save his life—and failed. Bull-terriers are much alike.

In olden days they fought the lion. the bear, and the bull. They and the hooligan earned a living together. So they gained an evil reputation !

Bull-terriers are white ; there is also a coloured Bull-terrier, not so powerfully built. The head is curiously shaped, nearly oval ; and the muzzle and forehead are practically on the same line (i.e. little or no ' stop '). The eyes are black and alert, and the dog is very broad across the chest and powerfully built. The tail is short, thick at the start, gradually tapering off to a fine point. Once upon a time short faces were desired, now the face is long. Height at shoulder 18 inches ; weight about 50 lb.

The coloured Bull-terriers are becoming popular. The white are liable to deafness, whilst the Staffordshire Dog, the brindle or fawn variety, is free from this trouble.

THE BULL-TERRIER (Miniature)

Same as above, but less than 12 lb.

THE BULL-TERRIER

The Bull-terrier was made from the Bulldog towards the end of the eighteenth century, for the Bulldog was found too slow in the dog-fighting pits, although its strength and courage were greatly to its advantage. Therefore, it was attempted to produce a breed of dog that had some of the quick movements of the Terrier and retained the strength and fighting powers of the Bulldog. That this attempt proved remarkably successful can be judged from the illustrations of such dogs which appeared in the Press from time to time. In *Sporting Life* two such dogs are shown, father and son, of the fighting strain, known as the *Paddington* strain, which at that time was renowned.[1] These dogs have a body shaped somewhat similar to that of the Bull-terrier of to-day, but their heads are of quite a different type, having what is known as the Bulldog head, better described as the head of the old-fashioned Mastiff. The weight is given as 70 lb., and, according to the note on the illustration, these two dogs have never been beaten, the elder dog having killed two dogs in its time.[2] They were immensely strong, and very agile, and great fighters. Whilst most of these Bull-terriers are shown as white with patches of other colour, few were actually pure white, and quite a number were to be seen black-and-tan. This fighting dog was associated with the fashionably attired young man of the day, who simulated the prize-fighter and booth-frequenter, with whom the Bull-terrier was a dog of all importance. On their excursions and visits to the taverns such gentlemen had usually one or more such dogs with them, and, apart from impromptu meetings in the roads or in a country village square or in a tavern yard, frequent dog-fighting meetings were arranged to take place in London[3] and at important towns. Whilst the Bull-terrier was more or less entirely a fighting dog, it was also tried out in the pits on bears and lions, and not infrequently on badgers, foxes, old horses, and donkeys, depending on what animal was obtainable for sporting purposes. The Bull-terriers also gained a reputation for their astonishing ability in killing rats in the rat-pits ; so, because of one thing and another, the Bull-terrier became the sporting dog. Whilst great was its popularity, Mr. Hinks, with whom we have dealt previously, all at once surprised Bull-terrier owners by bringing to their notice a new kind of Bull-terrier, which he had obtained by crossing his dogs with the smaller Old English White Terrier. This was the beginning of a new history of Bull-terriers, for it is from these improved Bull-terriers produced by Mr. Hinks that the present-day breed is descended. The owners of the old breed were

---

[1] A play-bill of 1819 advertised a match between two dogs, the property of a sporting nobleman, weighing 43 lb. each, to take place at the Westminster Pit, for 100 guineas, as a contest between " the famous white bitch of Paddington whose wonderful performances are so well known to require no further comment," and a brindle dog, of Cambridge, " a remarkable and well-known favourite, as his form bears extensive proof."   [2] See Plate 8, No. 4.

[3] So popular were these dog fights that to fail to know the name of a Bulldog was to prove oneself out of touch with the world's affairs. Jesse tells us that a relative, while riding through Wednesbury, stopped at the toll-gates on hearing the church bells ringing and asked the reason. " Old Sal's brought to bed ! " came the answer. Being none the wiser, he inquired who this " Old Sal " might be. " ' Old Sal ' ! ' Old Sal ' ! " repeated, the man as if addressing a deaf person, " don't you know who ' Old Sal ' is ? "   Then the toll-keeper explained that " Old Sal," a somewhat ancient but celebrated Bull-bitch, had just borne her first litter of puppies, and the bells were sending glad news around the countryside. (From *Dogs, their History and Development.*)

compelled to view the newcomers with certain interest, although to their minds the new breed was meet to be treated with ridicule, for its smaller size and less weight made it evidently a breed of no value as a fighting dog. It is unlikely that they would have taken much notice of it at all had it been bred or introduced by anyone except Mr. Hinks. But as things were the new breed was to be taken seriously. They admitted the dog was a prettier dog, but said quite openly that it was quite unsuitable for fighting. Mr. Hinks denied that his new breed was incapable of doing well in the dog-pit, and to substantiate his opinion offered to wager a case of champagne and a £5 note on one of his new Bull-terriers, stating that it would beat any dog of the old and heavier breed ! Such a challenge was hurriedly accepted, and the fight was staged at Bill Tuppers, in Long Acre. Mr. Hinks was represented by *Puss*, and in thirty minutes the fight was over and *Puss*, little the worse for the struggle, was the victor, and the old type Bull-terrier was dead. Such an end as that could only have one effect. From then onwards the new breed replaced the heavier breed, and the demand for the new breed developed rapidly, for it so happened that a few days later, or it may have been the next day, *Puss* appeared at the Cremorne Show, where she won second prize to her kennel brother, *Madman*.[1] Although hailed as " the new breed," and though certainly it was of a distinctive type, the Bulldog was not as much eliminated as it is to-day, for both *Puss* and *Madman* (who may, as I have stated, be taken to be progenitors of the modern Bull-terrier) had shorter faces and " *more lip* " than is to be seen in the present-day dog, and, moreover, they showed the Bulldog in their forelegs. It is clear that Mr. Hinks visualised something even less Bulldog-like than his famous *Puss* and the first *Madman*, for he continued to improve the type, always eliminating Bulldog and always retaining the leading kennel. How these dogs were bred, and their relationship, will never be known, for Mr. Hinks had the habit of using one name for more than one dog, and his favourite name for dog was *Madman*. So a *Madman* was to be found in his kennel, although not often was it the same dog. As to how the new breed was made, Mr. Hinks merely admitted using the small White English Terrier, but there was every reason to believe, although it was denied, that the new breed contained Greyhound blood, from which much quality would naturally result. *Jim Hinks,* as he was popularly known, continued to win the prizes, each dog he brought out having less of the wide mouth of the old type of Bull-terrier. The nostrils were no longer so large, and the skull and face had become longer. There was also a marked difference in the eyes, for the large open eye of the old type now had given way to Jim Hinks' *new-breed's eye,* small and half closed, as may be seen in *Landseer's* well-known picture, *Low Life.* Changes in the history of the breed were soon to come, for Mr. Hinks' continued success brought buyers, and he eventually sold his kennel to Mr. Sam Handley, on behalf of Mr. Ryder, of Sale, near Manchester. Mr. Ryder then sold the kennel to a Mr. Smythe, of Timperley, Manchester. These sales caused many others to go in for the breed, but the purchasers of Mr. Hinks' stock did not have matters their own way by any means, as they anticipated. For although Mr. Hinks had sold the pick of his kennel, he managed to produce a new *Madman*, which he named *Young Madman*, and was soon winning honours with it. *Victor*, a dog Mr. Hinks had bred, which had colour round one eye, and was on this account considered to be of little value, was offered for a time at a very low price. Nobody wanted him, and *Victor* might have ended his life as a waif in the streets if a certain judge had not bought the dog. Shortly afterwards the " mark-eye dog "

147

(*Victor* was known in this manner) appeared on the show bench, and, much to everybody's surprise, won first prize. It was openly said that the " mark-eye dog's " win was by arrangement, but this was soon proved to be incorrect, for wherever *Victor* appeared he won the leading prizes, until the year 1875, when his career was ended by poison at Hull Show.

The Kennel Club was soon to force the Bull-terrier into a definite position, and to cause the development of one size at the expense of the other sizes. Up to 1877 there had been two sizes of Bull-terriers. They had been some-what divided into the heavy-weight dog and the light-weight dog, the latter weighing under 16 lb., whilst the former dog weighed anything above 40 lb. In 1877 the Kennel Club instituted classes for Bull-terriers of about 24 lb. in weight, thus causing owners of heavy and light-weight dogs to concentrate entirely on the making of a dog suitable for such classes. In twenty years the heavy-weight and light-weight dogs were no longer to be seen. Further trouble was in store for the breed. It had been customary to crop all Bull terriers, a custom occasioned by the dog-pit, where an ear gave good purchase to an adversary's teeth, and being tender was likely to lead to the defeat of a dog thus taken advantage of. It was, therefore, found expedient to remove the greater part of the ear. The custom had continued after dog-fighting had fallen into disrepute. It must be here said that in 1895 a Mr. and Mrs. Carling and one other were summoned to appear for cruelty to a dog, in so much as they had cut off that dog's ears. This case became known as the Carling case. Although the dog on which they were arraigned was an Irish Terrier, the Bull-terrier breeders saw that if the Carlings were com-mitted to prison the cropping of Bull-terriers would also have to cease. The Bull-terrier Club therefore entered into the struggle, not only paying eight guineas towards the defence, but giving evidence at the hearing, and attempted to prove by witnesses that a Bull-terrier would *not be able to live at all* unless its ears were removed ![1]

The judge considered that evidence of this nature was not to be relied upon, and the Carlings were convicted. So seriously had the Bull-terrier breeders taken the conviction that we find it reported that the death knell of the breed had been struck. It certainly resulted in a somewhat difficult situation, and the Bull-terrier breeders were in a quandary, for whilst cropping ears might well take them to prison, no Bull-terrier that had whole ears was likely to win a prize ! It was not long, however, before the Bull-terrier breeders petitioned the Kennel Club, asking the Association to put a stop to the cropping of Bull-terriers ! In recent years the Bull-terrier has devel-oped yet further from the dog of the olden day and the dog of Mr. Hinks. It is believed that the Dalmatian was used between the time of Mr. Hinks and the present day, for some of the modern dogs revert to a Dalmatian type of head, and the ticking found prevailing in the Dalmatian occurs with fair frequency in Bull-terriers. Some are of the opinion that the now popular down face originated from a Collie cross. It is interesting to notice that the breed is becoming popular. Quite unjustly, it had for long suffered because of a reputation which was by no means of its own making ; it had also suffered because of a hereditary degeneration of a duct inside the ear which brought on deafness. As to deafness, the Bull-terrier breeders have taken the matter in hand. Some breeders (see note to illustrations) kill every dog that shows any sign of ear trouble. The Club expects its members to

---

[1] A dog's ears were cut to a particular pattern, and most frequently after cutting the ears were pinned or glued to a cork which was not removed until the ear had acquired the proper position.

adhere to a declaration which reads, that " all members of the Bull-terrier Club do undertake not to exhibit for competition deaf Bull-terriers," and, further, they agree to support the Club in every way to end the exhibiting of deaf dogs, whether they are owned by members or non-members. The result is that deaf Bull-terriers are less common, and there is every likelihood that within reasonable time deafness in the breed will be eliminated entirely.

THE BULL TERRIER.

Head : Appearance—Oval, almost egg-shape. Fairly long, but strength must not be sacrificed for length. Of considerable depth. Not too wide or coarse, and cheek muscles should not be prominent. Profile almost an arc from the occiput to the tip of the nose. The more downfaced the better. No **stop** or indentation. **Forehead :** Fairly flat and not domed between ears. The **occiput** not prominent. **Foreface :** Longer than the forehead and filled right up to the eyes, i.e., egg-like. **Muzzle :** Shows great strength and, though tapering, should not be "snipey." **Under-jaw :** Deep and strong. **Lips :** tight and clean. **Teeth :** Sound, strong, clean and perfectly regular. An undershot or overhung mouth is objectionable. **Ears :** Small and thin, situated on the top of the skull fairly close together. Erect or semi-erect. **Eyes :** Well sunken. As black as possible, with a piercing glint, giving a keen expression. Small, almond-shaped, or triangular. Nearer the ears than nose, set closely together, and obliquely placed. **Nose :** Black, with large well-developed nostrils. Bent downwards at the tip. **Neck :** Moderately long, tapering from shoulders to head. Very muscular, arched, and free from all traces of dewlap or throatiness. **Shoulders :** Strong and muscular, but without any heaviness or loading. Shoulder-blades wide, flat and sloping, well back. No slackness or dip at the withers. **Chest :** Broad, viewed from the front ; deep from withers to brisket. **Body :** Ribs well sprung, i.e., rounded ; back ribs deep. Intercostal muscles well developed. The back short, strong and muscular. No drop at withers. Only slightly arched at loin. **Legs :** Big-boned, but not coarse. **Forelegs :** Moderately high, perfectly straight, and the dog must stand well on them. The elbows not to turn outwards. Pasterns strong and upright. **Hindlegs :** Straight, viewed from behind. Thighs very muscular. Hocks well let down, and the bone to the heels short and strong. **Feet :** Round and compact, and the toes well arched ; resembling those of a cat, not a hare. **Tail :** Short, fine, set on low, and carried horizontally ; thick where it joins the body, and tapering to a fine point. **Coat :** Short, flat, rather harsh to the touch, and with a fine gloss. The skin fits the dog tightly. **Colour :** (For white)—Pure white coat. (For coloured and Staffordshire)—Colour (preferably brindle) to predominate. **General :** Strongly built, muscular, active, symmetrical, with a keen, determined expression. Full of fire, but of sweet disposition, amenable to discipline. **Faults :** Light bone. Legginess. Soft expression. Badly placed eyes. Light eyes. Domed skull. Butterfly nose. Pronounced cheekiness. Dished faced. Lippiness. Throatiness. Teeth not meeting evenly. Long and slack back. Long, thick, and gay tail. Loose shoulders. Loaded shoulders. Crooked elbows. Weak pasterns. Cow hocks. Big and splay feet. Toes turning either in or out. Soft coat. Long coat.

Narrow chest. Flat sides. Ewe neck. Markings on head and ticked coat. Rose or button ears. **Disqualifications :** Deafness. Wall eye. Wholly flesh-coloured nose. Markings behind the set on of head. **Preparation for the show :** The smellers, long eyebrows, and other long hairs on the head may be removed. The hair inside the ears clipped or shaved down to the true coat, not beyond. The long hair under the tail trimmed and the side thereof to proportion.

	POINTS.
Neck, shoulders, body and tail	20
Legs and feet	20
Head, skull, jaws, lips, teeth	20
Eyes and expression	15
Movement	10
Condition and pure white body	10
Ears	5
	100

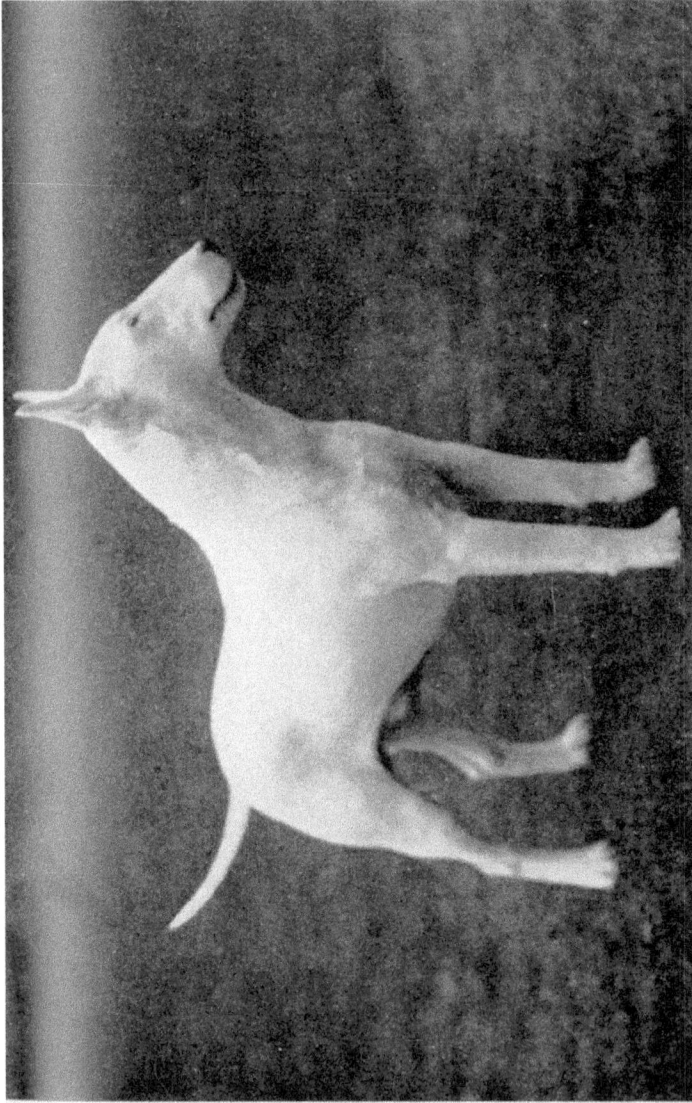

[Photo]

BULL TERRIER : Champion *Howsden Bail-Fire*, bred and owned by Miss M. L. Grey of Howsden Kennels, Flodden Edge, Cornhill-on-Tweed, Northumberland.

[Fall

THE BULL TERRIER

Origin and History.—It was the most natural thing in the world for those who wanted an indomitable dog possessing the indifference to pain and absence of fear shown by the bulldog combined with greater activity to experiment in crosses between the bulldog and a terrier. In all probability, these crosses were first made to a considerable extent about the end of the eighteenth century, when the progeny were often known as bulldog terriers. Sir Walter Scott was much attached to one named Camp :

> " The cleverest dog I ever had," he once wrote, " was what is called a bulldog terrier. I taught him to understand a great many words, insomuch that I am positive the communication between the canine species and ourselves might be greatly enlarged. . . . Towards the end of his life, when he was unable to attend me while I was on horseback, he generally watched for my return, and when the servant used to tell him his master was coming down the hill, or through the moor, although he did not

153

use any gesture to explain his meaning, Camp was never known to mistake him, but either went out at the front to go up the hill, or at the back to get down to the moorside."

In considering the Bull Terrier as we know him to-day, we have to remember that the Bulldog which had a share in his paternity was very different from his descendants of the present time, being higher on the leg and more actively built. Indeed, in the third edition of " Stonehenge," dated 1879, the Bulldog there depicted has a body that would do credit to any Bull Terrier, and he also has the long tail carried very much Bull Terrier fashion. At one time, no doubt, any plucky terrier was used, and the primitive Bull Terriers were fallow, smut, red or brindle in marking. The old sporting magazine of 1830 to which previous reference has been made stated that the taller variety of Scottish Terriers produced the best Bull Terriers.

The advent of dog shows produced a desire for a smarter and more shapely dog, and the late Mr. James Hinks of Birmingham addressed himself to the task of making a strain of white Bull Terriers with longer heads and more shapely bodies. For this purpose, presumably, he used the white English Terrier, which I regret has now disappeared. It would be idle to follow the evolution of the breed from its raw state into the smart animal with which we are familiar, but there is more than a suspicion that Dalmatian blood was used.

In the middle of last century it must be admitted that the Bull Terrier was a somewhat disreputable character, being chiefly celebrated for the celerity with which he killed rats in a pit. At an earlier date he was principally a fighting dog matched against others of his kind. The disappearance of his shady past has not affected his temperament. His disposition is to tackle anything that attacks his master. Bull Terriers are very popular among sporting men in India and other tropical countries. In Malaya packs are employed in hunting the wild boar, English dogs of most approved show pedigrees being among them. Mr. Marcuswell Maxwell, a sportsman resident in Kenya, who recently published some remarkable photographs of African big game, mentions that in one place :

> " during the day a big elephant which we were seeking wandered into our camp and terrified the cook, but it was summarily ejected by my Bull Terrier, whose bark frightened it."

All who have an eye for form and symmetry will appreciate the Bull Terrier at his best, but I must confess that there are more blanks than prizes in the breeding lottery, many being seen that are too long and weak in the back or that have very indifferent fronts, but the difficulties should merely be an incentive to strive after the best. When the ideal dog comes, he is something of which to be proud.

Mr. H. T. W. Bowell, who did so much to revive the fortunes of the breed in modern times when he took on the secretaryship of the Bull Terrier Club, once sent me some verses that appeared on a stud card issued by Mr. Wex Jones, an American breeder. They were called " The White Cavalier " :

> " There's a snow-white dog with a coal black eye,
> Whose temper is true as his courage is high,
> He's the last in a scrimmage and the last one that stops,
> For when he does fight he fights till he drops.
> He knows nothing of meanness and nothing of fear,
> For a gentleman's heart has the White Cavalier.
>
> He stands like a boxer : firm, active, and keen,
> With his punishing jaw, long, powerful, and clean.
> He's up on his toes, all ready to go,
> Like the flash of a gun, to meet playmate or foe.
> He's as strong as a bulldog, as fast as a deer,
> There's no dog with the dash of the White Cavalier.

The Bull Terrier, faithful and friendly, is so high-spirited and powerful that it is necessary to train him carefully when he is young, otherwise he will get out of hand and be a nuisance rather than a pleasure. He is one of the few dogs that will kill a cat at sight. A friend of mine who has a paddock at the back of his house much frequented by neighbouring cats once told me that his had killed nine in a week. Obviously then, it is necessary to accustom young Bull Terriers to cats before they acquire the propensity for slaying.

Until 1898 it was the custom to crop Bull Terriers, and when the Kennel Club prohibited the practice, it was thought they had dealt a deathblow to the breed. However, things did not turn out so badly as the pessimists predicted, but even now it is not always possible to get pleasing ears that are in keeping with the rest of the head. Latterly attempts have been made, with varying degrees of success, to revive the coloured dogs, a few of which have approached the whites in quality, but there is a long way to go yet before the ideal is attained. Deafness, a common fault in pure white dogs, used to be very general among Bull Terriers, but I do not think it is as prevalent now as it was at one time. For all that, anyone buying a puppy should examine him carefully.

Dr. G. M. Vevers, who has taken in hand the affairs of the Club, much to its advantage, has explained that deafness is a hereditary defect arising from the degeneration or entire absence of a small passage in the ear known as the cochlear duct. This form of deafness, he says, is almost certainly a Mendelian recessive, and if deaf specimens were destroyed or not used for breeding, the defect would in time die out.

Standard Description.— *Head*.—The kind of head desired in a Bull Terrier is best seen by reference to the diagram, p. 19. According to the standard of the Bull Terrier Club, it is of oval form, almost egg-shaped, fairly long, but strength must not be sacrificed to length. Of considerable depth, but not too wide or coarse, and the cheek muscles should not be prominent. The profile should be almost an arc from the occiput to the tip of the nose, the more down-faced the better, and there is no stop. The forehead should be fairly flat and not domed between the ears. Foreface longer than the forehead and filled right up to the eyes. The muzzle should show great strength, and though tapering should not be snipy. Under-jaw deep and strong. Lips tight and clean. Ears small and thin, fairly close together, erect, semi-erect, and placed on the top of the skull. Eyes well sunken, as nearly black as possible, small, almond-shaped or triangular, nearer the ears than the nose, set closely together and placed obliquely. Nose black. *Body.*—The neck must be moderately long, tapering from shoulders to head, very muscular, arched and free from all traces of throatiness. Shoulders strong and muscular, but without any heaviness or loading. No slackness or dip at the withers. Chest broad and deep from withers to brisket. Ribs well sprung and carried well back. Back short, strong and muscular, only slightly arched at the loin. *Legs.*—Legs big in bone but not coarse. Forelegs moderately long and perfectly straight. Pasterns strong and upright. Thighs very muscular. Hocks well let down. *Feet.*—Feet round and compact with the toes well arched. *Tail.*—Tail short, fine, set on low and carried horizontally, thick at the root and tapering to a fine point. *Coat.*—Coat short, flat, rather harsh to the touch and with a fine gloss. On show dogs the smellers, long eyebrows and other long hairs on the head may be removed ; the hair inside the ears can be clipped or shaved down to the true coat, the long hair under the tail may also be trimmed and the sides thereof to proportion.

Colour.—For whites, a pure white coat. For coloured and Staffordshire, colour (preferably brindle) to predominate. *Disqualifications.*—Deafness ; Wholly flesh-coloured nose ; Markings behind set-on of head.

THE BULL-TERRIER

THE Bull-terrier, as its name denotes, is mainly a cross between the bull-dog and the terrier, with a sprinkling of the pointer, mastiff, and greyhound added in order to improve them and produce a type of dog more to the ideals of those who have their interest at heart.

If we go back a century, we find Bull-terriers were despised, owing to the company they kept, as we are told that whenever you happened to drop across one, you usually found its owner to be a rogue. Charles Dickens, in his works, gave us an insight into the characteristics of the breed when he referred to one owned by Bill Sikes, and how he had trained it to serve him.

Many years ago the Bull-terrier took its place in the cockpit and prize-ring, and fully came up to expectations, for he could be well backed for sport in the pit; but in the year 1835 this pastime was made illegal by Act of Parliament, and from that date onwards breeders began to take a different outlook as to what type of dog to produce. Therefore the bull-dog element, which was at one period so pronounced, has been gradually reduced, and the terrier characteristics increased, while the fearless fighting spirit has been retained.

At one period the Bull-terrier was bred with black, fawn, or brindle markings, and the all-white specimens were unknown. Later on all-white dogs were frequently bred; but it was not until nearly sixty years ago that Mr. James Hinks, a dog-dealer in Birmingham, set the standard for the present-day type of dog, and to this day it is the nucleus of our best specimens.

Many of the old breeders objected to all-white dogs being produced, and claimed that the new blood which had been introduced to accomplish the object would affect the characteristics of the breed in general and do infinite harm, but it did not take long to prove the fallacy of this assumption; in fact, it was soon found that the all-whites were not only equal but superior to their predecessors.

The Bull-terrier is a lovable dog, and one of the most faithful breeds we have. He is playful with a child, and may be trusted in this direction. As a guard few are his equal. He is not boisterous or

A GENTLEMAN FIGHTER

BRITISH THROUGH AND THROUGH

TALE OF THE 50 50 DOG

THE BURGLARS ENEMY

A REAL BILL SIKES

BULL TERRIER
THE 50-50 DOG

clumsy, and is a very hardy animal. Unfortunately, many of them are born deaf, which is possibly accounted for by the fact that, prior to the English Kennel Club bringing in a rule to prevent cropping, this breed, like some of the other breeds with erect ears, had their ears cropped to enable owners to produce what they thought was a better ear carriage. Under these circumstances, when making a purchase, you should receive a guarantee that the dog is not deaf, as a specimen that is will be found useless as a guard, and a danger to himself and others.

THE BLUE PAUL FIGHTING DOG.

This variety of the Bull Terrier was bred in Scotland at one time. Mr. James B. Morrison was a leading breeder. The variety is extinct

Bull Terrier.—Those people whose hearts are warmed by the lovable qualities of the Bull Terrier are regarding with satisfaction the marked improvement that is taking place in the fortunes of this thoroughly genuine breed.

There is a good case to be made for the statement that the present popularity of the Bull Terrier, already greater and wider than at any other period of his history, is steadily increasing. The number of Bull Terriers registered annually at the Kennel Club, the increase in Challenge Certificates allotted to the breed, the growing entries at shows—all these facts speak of consistent progress. Indeed, at the Great Joint Terrier Show at Olympia in 1931 Bull Terriers delighted their own friends and dumbfounded the supporters of more fashionable breeds by achieving the largest entry in the show—223. It is no wonder that these dogs are far more frequently encountered in the streets nowadays, and that the Bull Terrier Club has not only in the last few years increased its membership from a problematical eighty to one of over 250, but is, probably, one of the richest dog clubs in the canine world.

Credit for this eminently impressive state of affairs may be equally divided between the improved quality of the dog himself and the selflessness, resource and energy of the Club's honorary secretary, Dr. G. M. Vevers, and his able assistant, Miss T. E. Salter. Bull Terrier enthusiasts are extremely fortunate in the work done on their behalf by Dr. Vevers, who, by conducting the breed's affairs with wisdom and far-sightedness, won for it the high respect that it at present commands.

If there is one regret more than another amongst those with an accurate knowledge of dogs, it is the atmosphere of suspicion that in the past has clouded the ordinary man's judgment of this fine and wholly British breed.

It used to be a grievance of the ignorant that this dog is quarrelsome, whereas in reality he is a sober-minded animal, slow to anger ; and who shall condemn him if, being roused, he bears himself manfully in the fight ? Surely the ability to defend oneself is a matter of allure rather than alarm. The truth is that the modern Bull Terrier, while retaining all his old unquenchable spirit, is no longer the ugly ferocious Bill Sykes dog that was bred for battling to death in the pits, for breeders have achieved remarkable success in retaining and developing only the best points of this lovable animal's ancestors. In fact, he is a real dog and a man's dog, combining all that is best of the two breeds from which he has been evolved, and displaying the exaggerations of neither.

Equally immoderate is the uninformed accusation of deafness, whereas, in fact, deafness in the breed amounts to no more than two per cent, and is steadily growing less ; and it seems to be forgotten that, owing to lack of pigment, all white animals—white mice, white cats, etc.—display this tendency towards deafness. Dr. Vevers himself has with his customary thoroughness established the responsibility for such occasional deafness that occurs, just as he has been adamant in insisting on the proper steps being taken for its suppression. He has no doubt that the lack of hearing associated with Bull Terriers and other animals deficient in pigment is an hereditary defect due to the degeneration or absolute absence of a small passage in the ear known as the cochlear duct. This form of deafness is almost certainly a Mendelian recessive, and he is of opinion that if all deaf specimens are killed as soon as the trouble is established, and if deaf sires and dams are not used for breeding purposes, deafness in Bull Terriers will die a natural death within ten to fifteen years.

This considered opinion has the official support of the Bull Terrier Club, who now require all new members to sign a declaration of honour that they will not exhibit, sell, or breed from deaf specimens ; and it is a fact that every reputable breeder destroys all deaf puppies as soon as possible. There cannot be much doubt that the strong action taken by the Bull Terrier Clubs of England and India in this matter has done much to stamp out one of the most deplorable infirmities from which any dog can suffer.

The original Bull Terrier, or Bull-and-Terrier, as he was then styled, bred for fighting in the pits, bore a far closer resemblance to the Bulldog of that day than to his Terrier forbears; for there exist scores of old prints as evidence that the old Bull-dog, as well as the Bull-

and-Terrier, had the unexaggerated (in comparison with the absurd modern standards) Bulldog head, and the legs, straight and longer, of the Terrier. At the same time that the new Bull-and-Terrier made its appearance, the Bulldog fanciers began breeding their animals heavier and lower to ground, so that the Bulldog acquired a new type and the Bull-and-Terrier, roughly speaking, and with the difference that his head was slightly longer, took the old type's place. Moreover, these Bull-and-Terriers, evolved by crossing Bulldogs with Terriers, mainly retained the colouring and markings of the Bulldog.

At the end of the 'fifties, however, a great and vital revolution was effected. Mr. James Hinks, of Birmingham, after years of experiment, burst upon an astonished and frankly sceptical world an entirely new animal —an immaculate white-coated Bull Terrier, from whom the undesirable points of the Bulldog (the roach back, the bent legs, the splay feet, the undershot jaw, etc.) were still further eliminated, and for whom he claimed equal courage and greater activity. The attractive appearance of the new dog in itself gave rise to a certain antagonism—it was considered that Mr. Hinks, in eliminating the Bulldog, had also eliminated its courage, and that the white Bull Terrier was altogether too "pretty" to hold its own in effective combat with the brindled and more pugilistic-looking heroes of so many fights. Mr. Hinks, however, found little difficulty in providing

SOME OF THE BEST.

Mrs. Adlam, owner of a noted kennel of Bull Terriers, which is one of the best in the world, with Ch. "Brendon Gold Standard" and Ch. "Brendon Beryl" with "Boomerang". Notice the ears and heads.

"OLD DUTCH".

The property of Mr. Hink, who made the modern type of Bull Terrier. "Old Dutch" was the best he ever had.

"NELSON".

In 1872 Mr. S. E. Shirley, President of the Kennel Club, bred Bull Terriers, and his "Nelson" was considered to be an outstanding example.

But this difficulty was rapidly and successfully tackled by breeders, and to-day the smart, naturally pricked ear is almost universal.

The introduction of quality into this breed has effected such progress that, both in appearance and characteristics, the Bull Terrier of to-day rightly has more friends than at any previous period in his history. From the point of view of looks, it is difficult to find a dog that satisfies the eye more completely than does the perfectly balanced Bull Terrier, standing as he does, or should, on the tips of his toes, with every steel-like muscle taut, his piercing little eyes and his tight-fitting skin combining with the proud lift of

practical demonstration of the error of these views and from that day the white Bull Terrier has steadily established and increased his excellence and his popularity.

Only when cropping of the ears was barred about 1895 was the success of the new breed threatened for since the new dog was eminently both gladiator and terrier, alertness of appearance was essential.

his head to intensify a picture of perfect physical fitness.

It is, however, the Bull Terrier's serenity of character and his unexpected gentleness that command respect and provide his greatest charm. Though he is possessed of invincible courage, he is rarely the aggressor in a fight, and to this slowness to anger, this lack of "nerves", is due the fact that he is probably the only terrier never known to snap; indeed, there is no breed of dog to whom the word "treacherous" is less applicable. Though his strength is exceptional, he makes the gentlest use of it The stronger the dog the gentler and more reliable he seems with all young things, whether they possess two legs or four; and it is probably just because the Bull Terrier has the blood of a thousand fighting ancestors in his veins that he can safely be left alone with a baby and will suffer himself to be killed rather than betray his trust.

A gallant, patient, sweet-dispositioned gentleman is this White Cavalier, and some think that he will eventually establish himself as the most desirable Terrier of all in the eyes of men and women who desire their dog to be a staunch friend, a true sportsman and an indomitable protector Nor is he any less human and lovable because he is sentimental; and, being little given to barking, he has silence as well as

THREE NOTED BULL TERRIERS OF YESTERDAY.

Mr. W. I. Pegg had a very strong winning kennel of Bull Terriers and was one of the most successful breeders. Here is his "Sherborne Queen", "Woodcote Teaser" and "Woodcote Tartar", at the end of the nineteenth century.

164

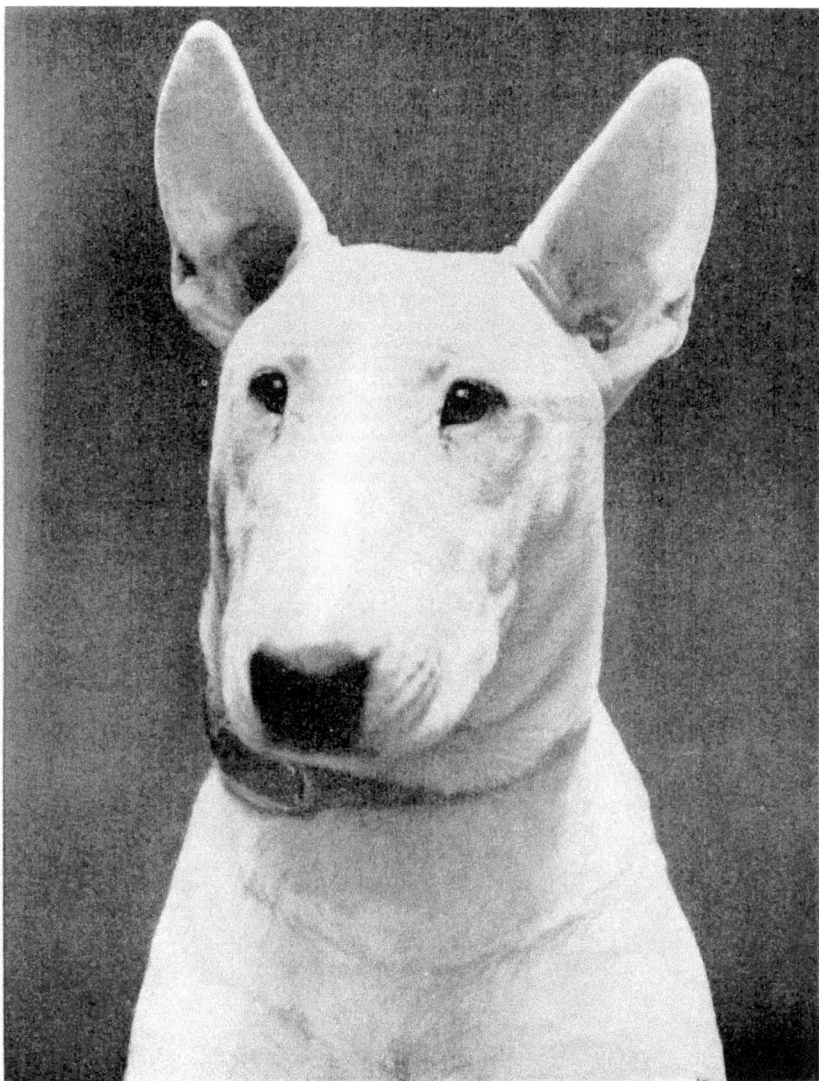

[Photo]
[Sport & General.

CH. "MITSU DANNEBROG".

Here we have the typical head of the Bull Terrier of 1934. The dog was bred by Major Mitford Brice. The reader's attention is drawn to the head of "Old Dutch" opposite.

strength to commend him. A hardy healthy active lovable old fellow

As material for future building the breed is fortunate in the continuance of famous strains and the possession of breeders of wide and established experience. No summary of Bull Terrier history would be complete without some reference to that fine old gentleman, Mr. Fred North, in whose character unvarying courtesy and utter devotion to the breed are there for all to see. It is not easy to speak, without being fulsome, of a man who showed his first dog in 1884 · who exhibited at St. Stephen's Hall at the first Cruft's show ever held ; who has owned a score of Champions who in 1933, at the age of 75, had a desperate illness, and who on recovery exhibited and handled at every available show ; who through all those years never found it possible to speak an unjust word of any man, and never failed to give encouragement to newcomers Mr North has a fine record. at all times a magnificent loser and a modest winner, and by the strength and charm of his character, commanding respect where others could not.

In Mrs Adlam, of the Brendon Kennels, the breed has been equally fortunate, for her helpfulness has become proverbial and her support of the Bull Terrier invaluable

BULL TERRIER MINIATURE. [E. C. Ash.
At the end of the nineteenth century Bull Terrier Miniatures were very popular and weighed from 4 to 8lb., and had the characteristics of the larger dog. To-day, as the illustrations in this work show, attempts are being made to rebuild the variety.

whose Cylva strain has contributed more towards the introduction of quality than any other factor, and whose judgment is unsurpassed ; Mr. W. J. Tuck of the Gladiator prefix, and through whose hands have passed many of the most famous dogs of olden times : Dr. G. M. Vevers, of "Regent" renown : Mr. H. K. McCausland, so quick at spotting promising youngsters ; Colonel and Mrs. Baldrey ; and Mrs. S. G. Yearsley, whose Ch. 'Black Coffee" is, in the opinion of many, the best dog of his period. There are also many others scarcely less renowned · to Miss M. L. Grey is due a real debt of gratitude for her Northumberland-bred Howsden dogs, while without Mr. Tom Gannaway the breed would lose half its attraction.

Her Ch."Rhoma" became the best Bull Terrier of modern times whose usefulness to the breed is exemplified by the fact that she gave birth to four champions. For this peerless bitch Mrs. Adlam refused £250.

Other famous breeders are Mr. Carleton Hinks, grandson of the founder of the white Bull Terrier; Mrs. D. H. Robbs,

Distinguished dogs are less easy to enumerate if only because the degree of distinction must inevitably be a matter of opinion. But since 1929 the following may be said to have been outstanding amongst "Classical Cotton'' : dogs' Ch. "Classical Cotton'' :

OF MORE THAN ORDINARY EXCELLENCE [E. C. Ash.
Ch. "Green-hill Wonder" was one of Mr. C. P. Lea's winning Bull Terriers at the end of the nineteenth century. She is described by Mr. Rawden Lee to have been of more than ordinary excellence.

[Photo] GOING UP FOR JUDGMENT. [Sport & General.

Whilst in the olden days dogs travelled in boxes, baskets, and even sacks to the various shows and newspaper correspondents went to them in fear and trembling), to-day they go on their way in cars, as do these Bull Terriers, "Jerry" and "Peg of Judington", the property of Mrs. Phillips.

Ch. "Regent Juno"; Ch. "Brendon Becky"; Ch. "Mitsu Dannebrog", who at $7\frac{1}{2}$ months won her first Certificate at the Great Joint Terrier Show where Bull Terriers topped the entry with a record of 223; Ch. "Brendon Barbed Wire" and Ch. "Isis 10". Amongst many celebrities whom I must necessarily omit are a number who have achieved fame abroad after exportation, chiefly animals from the kennels of Mrs. Adlam, Mrs. Robbs, and Mr. McCausland.

Miniature Bull Terriers up to 18 lb. have displayed a slight but not very decided improvement, and in the case of these small specimens there still seems to be some difficulty in approximating the real Bull Terrier type. Poor head qualities, and the lack of that fire that is so essential a feature of the breed, appear to stamp this variety; although the brindle miniature "Lone Knight" must be exempted from these two criticisms.

Present events abundantly show that the coloured Bull Terrier is not only achieving a wide popularity but is improving in quality, although it has to be admitted that his quality is at present far from equalling that of the whites; nevertheless, much is being accomplished in that direction. It is to be feared that the coloured dogs are, generally

CH. "RHOMA".

Although Bull Terrier fanciers usually prefer a pure white dog, and much colour places it among the Staffordshires, a patch round the eye is allowed, though at one time this created ill-feeling—so much so that one noted dog is reported to have been poisoned by an irritated rival breeder.

Ch. "Howsden Bailfire"; Ch. "Beshelson Bayshuck"; Ch. "Num Skull," the possessor of a phenomenal head and the winner of countless certificates; Ch. "Ringfire of Blighty"; Ch. "Black Coffee"; Ch. "Brendon Gold Standard". Of a large number of successful stud dogs, I have only space to quote "Galalaw General", Ch. "Cylva General", "Regent Pluto" and "The Sheik of Chartham".

Outstanding amongst bitches during the same period are the following: Ch. "Silver Belle," a perfect but unusually small specimen; Ch. "Trafgar Winalot"; Ch. "Lady Winifred", the first and so far only coloured champion, although there is no doubt that, had he lived, the magnificent red dog "Hunting Blondi" must have achieved champion status; Ch. "Rhoma", in my opinion the queen of them all; Ch. "Pamela Skellum";

Photo]　　　　　CH. "BUTTERFLY WHITE BUD".　　　　　*[Fall.*

That the breed has not altered in recent years except to acquire greater quality may be noticed by comparing this champion of past days with dogs illustrated on other pages.

168

speaking, less reliable in temper than the whites, and the multiplicity of colours offers a problem that will require attention before long. Brindle dogs are acceptable ; red dogs are understandable ; but parti-coloured dogs of black-and-tan-and-white and other variations of the rainbow are as difficult to harness to the imagination as is the rainbow to the earth. Nevertheless, from the show point of view these dogs must be judged as Bull Terriers, and should not be penalized for any eccentricity of colour scheme.

But whether immaculately white or handsomely brindle, to those who desire their dog to be in no sense commonplace; to those who want him to be a staunch friend, a true sportsman and a courageous defender; and to those who require that their pet should combine strength with endurance, gentleness with friendship, and protection with loyalty, the Bull Terrier is confidently commended.

POINTS OF THE BULL TERRIER.

The forehead fairly flat and shorter than the foreface. The foreface filled right up to the eyes. The muzzle strong, with deep underjaw and tight lips. Teeth even. The undershot jaw of the Bulldog is anathema. Ears small and erect on top of the skull. Eyes are most important, as giving the character of the breed. These should be small, well sunken, and dark ; and they should be almond-shaped or triangular and placed obliquely and close together, nearer the ears than the nose. The resulting expression should be a piercing, rather wicked glint. A soft expression in a Bull Terrier is as inappropriate as scented hair on a boxer.

THE NECK should be moderately long, tapering from shoulders to head. Muscular, arched, and free from throatiness.

THE SHOULDERS strong and muscular but not heavy. Shoulder blades wide, flat and sloping well back. No dip at withers.

THE CHEST broad viewed from the front and deep from withers to brisket.

A PROMINENT SPORTSMAN.
Sir Harry Preston, a great lover of dogs, always had a special liking for the Bull Terrier and has here posed for his photograph with his favourite dog.

TYPE.—The Bull Terrier is the gladiator of the canine race, and should be a strongly built, muscular, active, symmetrical animal, with a keen, determined expression. Full of fire, but of sweet disposition and amenable to discipline.

THE HEAD.—Almost egg-shaped. Fairly long provided strength is not sacrificed to length. Deep, but not too wide or coarse. Cheek muscles not prominent. The profile, without a stop, should be almost an arc from occiput to nose.

THE BODY should have well-sprung ribs ; a short, strong and muscular back ; and only a slight arch at loin.

THE LEGS should be strong boned but not coarse, the front legs not too high and perfectly straight. A Bull Terrier should stand well on his feet and be low to ground. The elbows must not turn outwards and the pasterns must be strong and upright.

169

CH. "BRENDON BERYL".

This is one of Mrs. Adlam's noted bitches, and its longer legs and general difference in build will be recognized in comparison with "Num Skull".

THE FEET should be cat's feet, round and compact, with the toes well arched.

THE TAIL is required to be short, tapering, set on low, and carried horizontally.

THE COAT has to be short, flat, ather harsh, but with a fine gloss. A Bull Terrier's skin should fit him tightly.

COLOUR for whites is pure white, with the exception of permissible markings on the head. Markings behind the set-on of head are disqualifications.

FAULTS OF THE BULL TERRIER.

Light bone. Legginess. Soft expression. Badly placed eyes. Light eyes. Domed skull. Butterfly nose. Pronounced cheekiness. Dish-faced. Lippiness. Throatiness. Unevenly meeting teeth. Long and slack back. Long, thick and gay tail. Loose shoulders. Loaded shoulders. Crooked elbows. Weak pasterns. Cow-hocks Big and splay feet. Toes turning either in or out. Soft coat. Long coat. Narrow chest. Flat sides. Ewe neck. Ticked coat.

DISQUALIFICATIONS.

Deafness Wall-eye. Wholly flesh-coloured nose. Markings behind the set-on of head.

Bull Terrier (Coloured).—The Coloureds are descended from the old breed of Staffordshire Bull Terriers, and from the modern Pure White Bull Terrier. The Staffordshire was bred to fight in the pits in the days when staged dog-fights were a national amusement. They were much smaller and lighter than the modern White Bull Terrier, and entirely different in type, having short heads and thick skulls. They were all colours; every shade of brindle and brindle-and-white, fawn and fawn-and-white, seem to have been the most common.

The Pure White Bull Terrier was standardized many years ago by the late Mr. James Hinks, of Birmingham, and has now been bred to a high state of perfection. It was the blending of these two, the Pure White and the Staffordshire, that produced the modern Coloured Bull Terrier.

The breeder's ideal is a dog as good in type and quality as the best Pure White, but with the Coloured coat of the Staffordshire. To do this, the best Staffordshires available were mated to the finest Pure Whites. The results were an immediate improvement in type. Again, the

CH. "NUM SKULL".

It is difficult in a few words to describe the correct Bull Terrier and just as difficult to point the faults of an excellent specimen. Even champions vary to some extent, as will be seen if we compare Mr. H. L. Summer's "Num Skull" with the picture above.

171

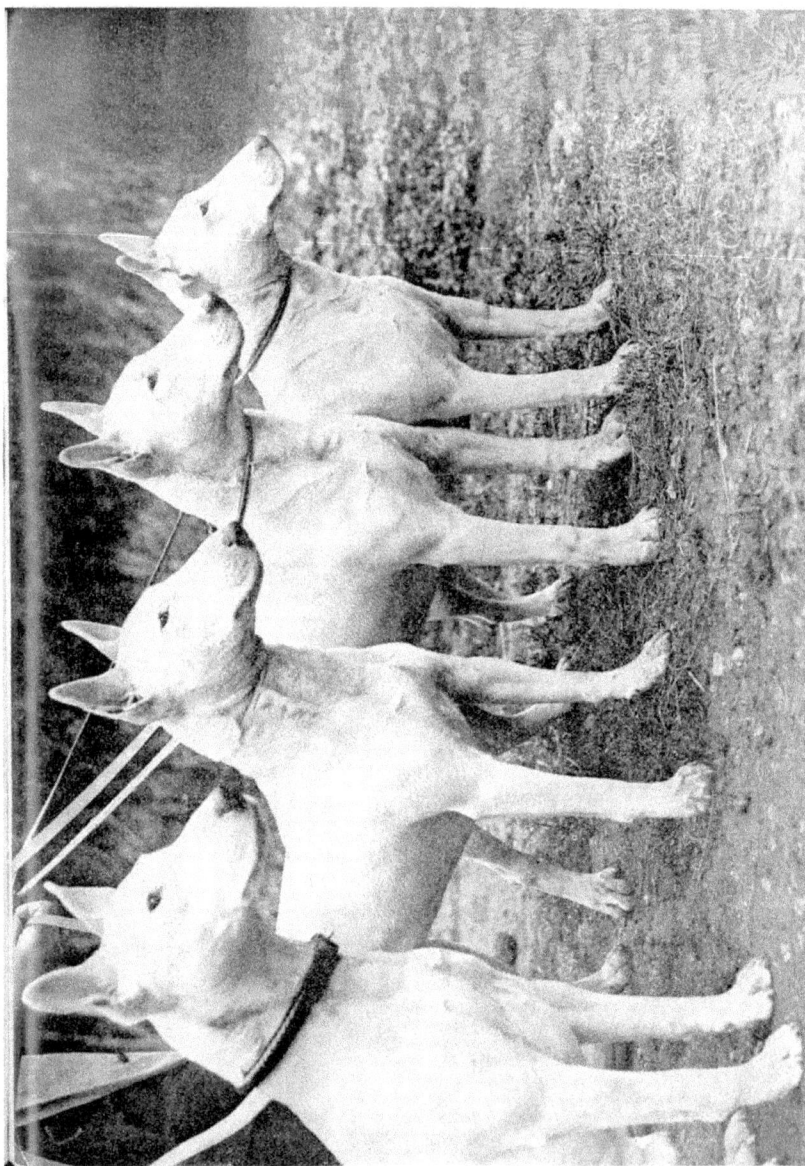

A TEAM

There is nothing very much nicer than to see several dogs of the same variety standing side by side; and it is particularly interesting to a breed such as the Bull Terrier, for it allows comparison. Mrs. Yearsley's Bull Terriers are seen here.

A FAVOURITE.

"Bullterrier Rhoda" is said to have the finest eye expression seen for many a long day. "Rhoda" owned by Miss E. M. Weatherill, is being held by Miss Joan Melville, the noted actress.

most typical specimen was selected, and again mated to a quality dog, and so on. But it was not a fast improvement, as breeders had continually to return to the Staffordshire for the desired colour. so losing a little of the type already gained.

The first Coloured dog to win a Kennel Club Challenge Certificate was "Bing Boy", a brindle-and-white, bred by Mr. Sievier. He won his first Certificate under Count V. C. Hollender at the Great Joint Terrier Show in 1919, and a second later on. The next Coloured to make a name on the show bench against the pick of the Whites was Mr. Dockerill's Ch. "Lady Winifred", an outstanding brindle-and-white bitch This was ten years after "Bing Boy". She won her first Certificate in 1929 at the Great Joint Terrier Show under Major Owen Swaffield, her second at the National Terrier Show in 1931, and her third at Cruft's in 1931. She thus became a full champion, and at that time was the only Coloured dog or bitch to have this achievement to her credit. The third outstanding Coloured to be benched, and in the opinion of many the best ever seen, was a brilliant red-and-white dog, "Hunting Blondi", bred by Mrs. Ellis. He won his first Certificate at the National Terrier Championship Show under Count V. C. Hollender, and a second at Taunton under Major Owen Swaffield. He was Reserve for the Certificates at Cruft's, and at the Great Joint Terrier Show in 1931. He would undoubtedly have

ONE OF THE BEST.
Breeders are striving for perfection as seen by this specimen.

Photo]   *[Sport and General.*
BULL TERRIER TYPE.
"Cyivia Bubbles", the property of Mr. F. North shows clearly the Bull Terrier type.

Photo]   *[Fall.*
CH. "BRENDON GOLD STANDARD".
This dog, the property of Mrs. Adlam, is claimed to have been the most typical and up-to-date Bull Terrier in 1933.

become a full champion but for his death when under two years of age. His early death was a misfortune to the Coloureds as he would have been a valuable sire.

The fourth Coloured dog who deserves special mention is Mr. J. S. Symes' brindle dog, "Nelstan Cotton". This dog won a Certificate at the Metropolitan and Essex Championship Show in 1932, under Count V. C. Hollender, and was Reserve for the honour at Manchester Championship Show in 1933. He holds a very fine show record—shown against the Whites as well as in Coloured classes, he has never, with the exception of one occasion, been unplaced at Championship and Open Shows. He has also done well at stud, Mr. R. H. Glyn's "Tigress of Blighty" (brindle) and Miss P. K. Timins' "Boko's Double" (brindle-and-white) both big winners, owning him as sire.

Other present-day brindle dogs worthy of mention, who have made names for themselves in the show-ring, and who are further proving their worth as successful sires are: Mrs. Horton's "Batchworth Barrister" (brindle-and-white), Mrs. Robbs' "Tiger of Blighty" (brindle), Captain and Mrs. Strettell's "Cheddington Warrior" (brindle-and-white, litter brother to "Nelstan Cotton") and Miss D. Montague Johnstone's "Romany Radium" (brindle-and-white).

At one time it was not easy to get Coloured classes scheduled, even at the major events, and the breeders themselves had to guarantee to pay any losses which might be incurred through lack

174

ol entries. And pay they nearly always did as at that time there were rarely sufficient dogs benched to cover the prize money. It is at this point in the development of the breed that breeders **really** started to study seriously the question of colour ratios ; how to produce the particular colours they wanted without sacrificing type or quality. The breed as a whole had advanced very definitely in type, and quality generally was noticeably improved. Show specimens were still few in number, but the general type was such that there was no question of having to go back to the Staffordshire again. There was plenty of Coloured dogs, Colour-bred—not Staffordshire-bred—available for breeding. Careful study of the law of colour inheritance and the keeping of very accurate records brought the following invaluable facts to light ·

On Producing the colour Brindle—Breeders are almost unanimous in agreeing that the brindle colour is the most desirable. The specification of a Coloured Bull Terrier is "Any Colour, other than White," and "White not to Predominate". This means that show Coloureds can be any colour . brindle, brindle-and-white, red, red-and-white, fawn, fawn-and-white, black, black-and-white, providing only that the colours, and not the white markings, shall predominate. Actually, brindle and brindle-and-white are unquestionably

Photo] *[Fall.*
CH. "BRENDON BERYL".
A head-study of this well-known champion, bred by Mrs. Adlam. Notice the eye expression and shape of head.

the most popular from the show point of view, and are undoubtedly, as will be shown, the most valuable for breeding purposes. The all important fact now put forward with regard to this colour is . That to breed brindles, it is necessary that one of the parents should be brindle. Until this theory was made known, it was considered quite possible to get brindle puppies from two parents. neither of which were brindles themselves, but which were brindle-bred. Example : If the sire used was red, out of brindle parents, and the bitch also red (or fawn or black), but also out of one or two brindle parents, it was considered quite reasonable to expect a proportion of brindle puppies in the resulting litter, especially as it is known that puppies frequently resemble their grandparents considerably more than their sire and

Photo] *[Fall.*
CH. "BRENDON BARBED WIRE".
On page 255 we give the head of this dog and here is a picture of him showing his remarkable type. His shoulders neck body and chest are particularly fine.

"BRENDON BLONDE VENUS",
Bred by Mrs. Adlam and owned by Captain Goldsmith. "Blonde Venus" in 1934 was considered one of the best Coloured Bull Terrier bitches exhibited.

"BRENDON DRAGON",
Mrs. G. M. Adlam's remarkable brindle dog won the Lady Winifred Challenge Cup for the best Coloured Bull Terrier at Cruft's in 1934.

176

dam. In practice, however, it is not so. Miss
Montague Johnstone, who has kept accurate
records of all matings, has never yet bred or seen
a brindle puppy produced from two non-brindle
parents.

Breeders should make it a firm rule to use one
brindle parent in all their matings. Not to do so
is to ask for disappointment. The fact is stressed
here, as novices taking up the breed without this
knowledge would become disappointed and dis-
couraged at their inability to breed this most
popular and most saleable colour. It is also
necessary for the good of the breed, as constant
and continual non-brindle matings carried on on
a large scale would in time result in the loss of
the brindle colour, since it is by far the most elusive.

It has been proved, by a survey of hundreds
of litters, that the brindle colour does not appear
in equal ratio to the others, but considerably less
often. Reds and fawns appear almost exactly
as calculated. Black, being the strongest colour
of all, appears more often.

Reds, and Red-and-Whites.—This colour comes
second in popularity to the brindle. Although
not quite so popular in the show-ring, it runs a
very close second with the general public. The ideal
shade is a bright red, similar to the summer coat

on a chestnut horse, and it should look glossy
and shining. The almost whole-colour red has
nearly always a blackish mask, and is sometimes
called a "red-smut". The red-and-white often
shows no sign of a darker face colour, but carries
instead a white blaze, with white chest and feet.
A common fault of the reds is a light amber-
coloured eye. This is to be avoided on breeding
animals, as it is frequently passed on. It is a
thoroughly bad fault, and spoils the typical expression. On the other hand, a brilliant red, with
really dark little eye, is most attractive, and has
many admirers. The reds are not difficult to
breed, as they can be produced from any colour
combination : brindle to brindle, brindle to red,
black or white ; red to red, or to white, black or
fawn ; fawn to any colour, etc., can all produce
reds. Care should be taken not to introduce
too much white blood, as in this case the red will
lose its brightness and become pale and washed-
out looking.

Fawns, Fawn-and-Whites, Fawn-Smuts.—These
can be produced similarly to the reds, from any
combination of colours, and appear in about equal
quantities to the reds.

*Blacks, Black-and-Whites, Black-Brindles, Tri-
Colours.* — This class is not so popular as the

others, but can be very striking in appearance, and has quite a following. The coat should shine like black satin, and a dark eye is absolutely essential. A light eye shows up on this colour more than any other and is an abomination. It is doubtful if there is a completely black dog, though several breeders have been trying to produce an all-black specimen, and very handsome he would be. They are usually either black with white points, or black with white points and brindling on the cheeks and legs (black brindle), or tricolour (black, with white markings and tan points). It is interesting and important to note that the black-brindles can pass the brindle factor to their progeny, when mated to other-than - brindle bitches. The black - brindle should therefore always be chosen for breeding purposes 'when breeding from blacks, as they can rank as brindles from the breeding point of view though they will also undoubtedly produce a large proportion of their own colour. They are the easiest colour of all to breed, and turn up in large quantities in matings of all and every colour combination. Curiously enough, the more Pure White blood introduced, the greater the number of blacks produced. If one of the parents used is a Pure White, and the other parent fifty per cent white-bred, a good proportion of the resulting litter will almost certainly be black. The fact that the Pure White parent has no blacks in his pedigree and that the other parent has none for generations will not alter the fact. While dealing with this colour, mention must be made of Mrs. E. Mallam's outstanding black-brindle dog, "Isis Nap". He won a Challenge Certificate at Taunton Championship Show in 1933 under Mr. Holgate, and is the first of his colour to win a Certificate. He was Best Coloured Bull Terrier at the Great Joint Terrier Championship Show 1933, under Mr P B

Grain, and has distinguished himself elsewhere, only once being beaten by another Coloured dog.

Colour - Bred Whites.—"Colour-Bred Whites" is the name given to the white puppies which appear in large or small quantities in many litters produced by Coloured dogs. Every well-bred Coloured is more or less closely related to the Pure Whites, for, as already stated, the Coloured breeders use as much Pure White blood as is possible (without losing the coloured coat) in order to improve the type of their stock. It was thought, quite naturally, that the Colour-bred White, when mated to a Coloured dog, would produce a greater proportion of Coloured puppies in her litters than would a Pure White bitch. Some breeders are still of this opinion, but they cannot be certain. It is stated, by those who have studied the question, that the Colour-bred White breeds true to its coat, and when mated to Pure Whites never produces anything but white puppies This leads one to imagine that, mated to a Coloured, it would still breed true to its coat, and that the Coloured puppies in the litter owed their colour to the other parent. The whole question is still being investigated, and is as yet extremely vague. It is not advisable (in Miss Johnstone's opinion, though some breeders disagree) to keep these white puppies, except, of course, for experimental purposes. They are neither one thing or the other. They are obviously not as valuable as their Coloured litter brothers and sisters to the Coloured breeder, and the breeder of Pure Whites does not want them.

The Value of the Pure Whites in Breeding Show Coloureds, and the Disadvantages of Using them to Excess. — The Pure Whites are at a higher state of perfection as a whole than are the Coloured dogs. We therefore use them to lift the general type of the Coloureds up to their higher

"WURRICUE".
The Coloured Bull Terrier Miniature seems to be more of the Bull Terrier type than the White Bull Terrier Miniature.

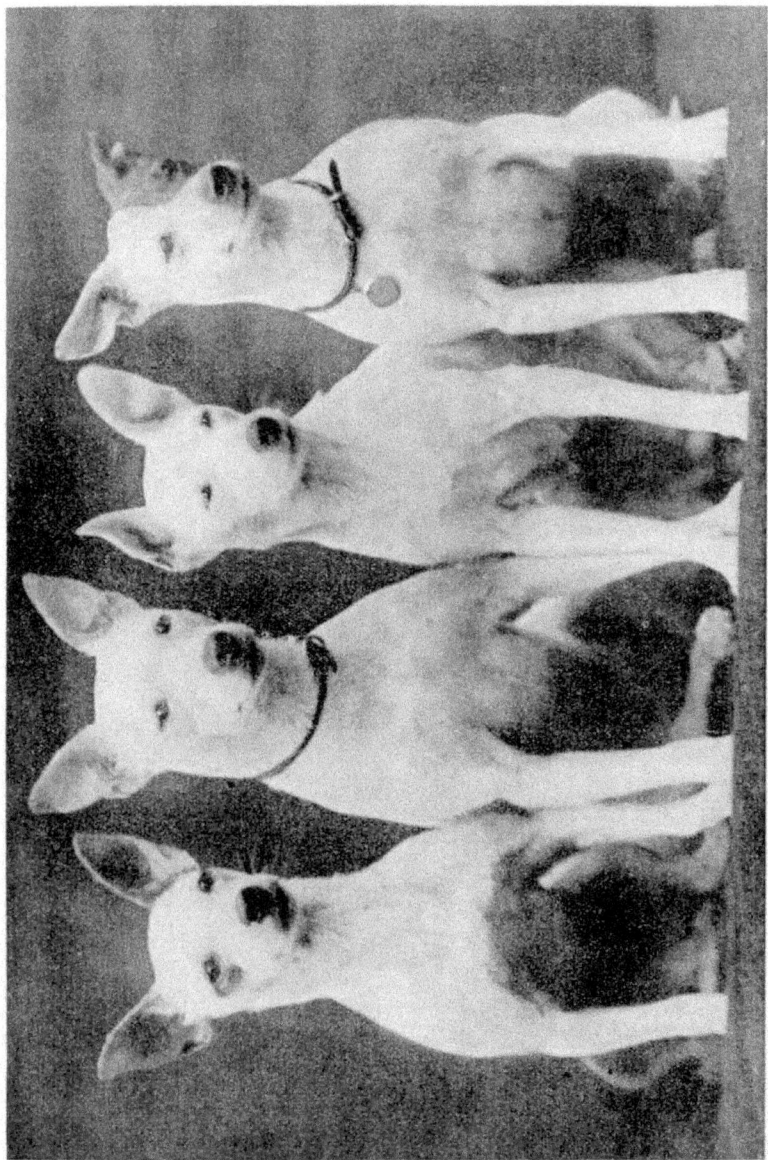

MINIATURE BULL TERRIERS. [Fall.

Attempts have been made to re-establish the Miniature Bull Terrier, so popular at one time, and here we have some of the breed prominent in 1933.

"ISIS NAP".
This is Mrs. Ernest Mallam's fine coloured Bull Terrier
"Isis Nap", a very useful specimen.

"BETTER LATE THAN NEVER!"
The alert expression of the Bull Terrier is here in evidence.
Could a dog's face exhibit more expression?

he should immediately put his bitches back to the best Coloured dog (preferably brindle) that he can find, and if he can find one to suit his bitch that is Colour-bred on both sides, as well as being Coloured himself, so much the better. He will then get back to properly marked, bright-coloured puppies, but of good type, since they are closely related to Pure Whites. It is better that the sire should be the White parent rather than the dam, when using a Pure White. A Coloured bitch, mated to a White, seems to produce a greater proportion of Coloured puppies, better marked, than vice versa.

level. Quality, we know, will be improved, but there are disadvantages if used too often : (1) We get too many Colour-bred Whites. (2) We get a far greater proportion of Blacks than we want. (3) We lose the Brindle colour. (4) The Coloured puppies that we do get will be badly marked, with too much white on them, such as white splashes on the back behind the shoulders, completely white face, etc., so that it can hardly be said of them with truth that white does not predominate. (5) The Reds and Fawns will lose their brightness and become pale and washed out. As soon as the breeder notices any of the above faults in his stock,

A CONSISTANT WINNER.
"Nightrider's Bronx Cocktail" won many prizes between 1927-1932. Three of his sons were exported to India.

180

MRS. MONTAGUE STURRIDGE AND HER BULL TERRIER.

Once upon a time the Bull Terrier was a breed debarred from society because it was associated with the gamester, pugilist, and dog-fighter; but to-day the Bull Terrier is a member in leading households.

From Hobday's "Surgical Diseases of the Dog and Cat". By courtesy of Messrs. Baillière, Tindall & Cox.

CROPPING.

The left hand photo shows the ears carried naturally; whilst that on the right shows how they appear after "cropping" has been performed

THE BULL TERRIER   CH. BUBBLES GIFT

THIS is a breed of dog which at a first glance warns off a prospective owner, but its expression is very misleading, for a greater-hearted dog does not exist.

Many people are under the misapprehension that this breed is dull-witted and deaf, but such is far from being the case. It is very slow to anger, although if attacked it can give more than is given.

The breed was immortalized by Charles Dickens when he created the character of "Bill Sykes," the Bull Terrier being the "tyke." The type of to-day has much in common, but it is by no means as ugly or ferocious as that depicted.

It is well known that a similar dog to the Bull Terrier was evolved and used by our forbears for bear-baiting and other forms of this so-called "sport."

White is the usual colour of the coat, but the new-coloured variety have a definite following.

THE BULL TERRIER (old type)   BILL LAZELL

THE BULL TERRIER (old type)   BILL LAZELL

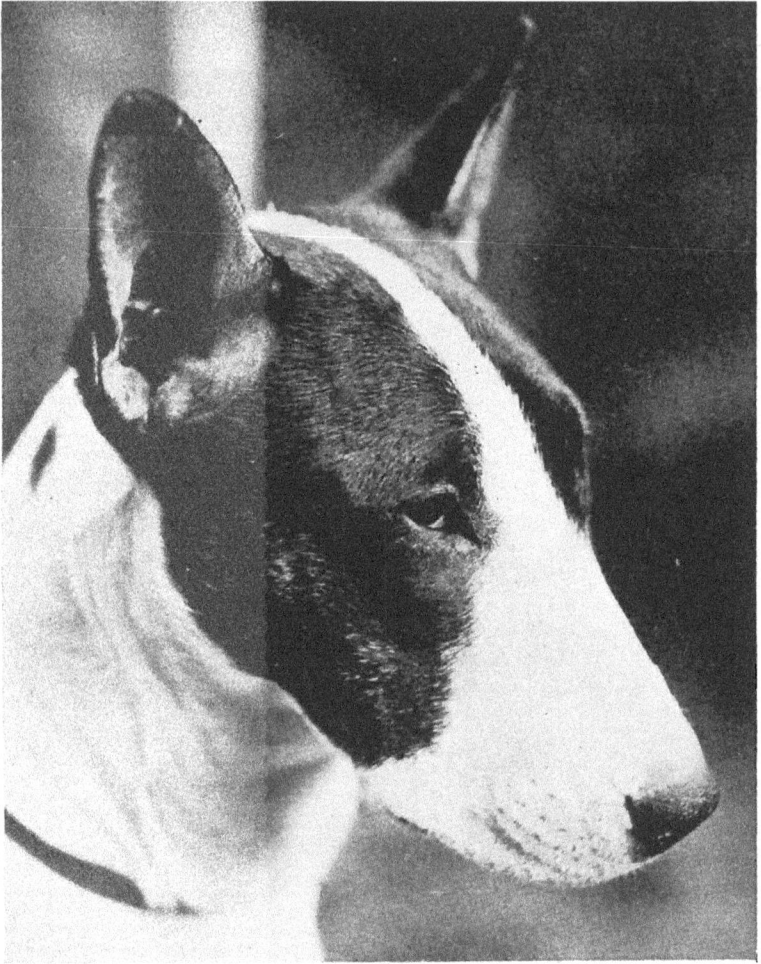

THE BULL TERRIER

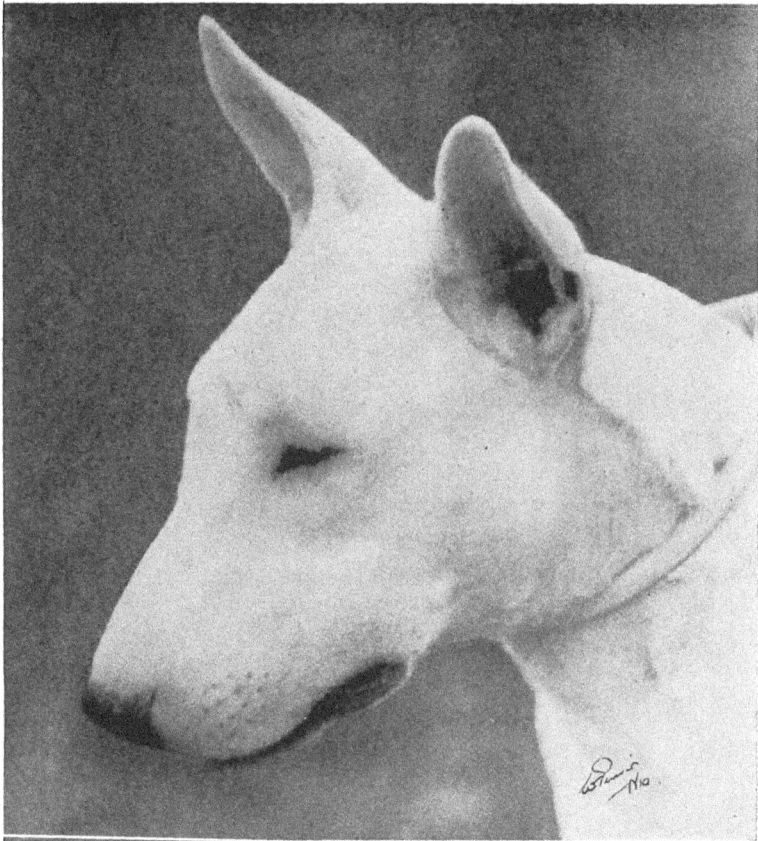

THE BULL TERRIER   CH. BUBBLES GIFT

187

THE MINIATURE BULL TERRIER WURRICOE

THE BULL TERRIER

The HEAD—APPEARANCE : Oval, almost egg shape. Fairly long, but strength must not be sacrificed for length. Of considerable depth. Not too wide or coarse, and cheek muscles should not be prominent. PROFILE : Should be almost an arc from the occiput to the tip of the nose. The more down-faced the better. No stop or indentation. FOREHEAD : Fairly flat and not domed between ears. The occiput not prominent. FOREFACE : Longer than forehead and filled right up to the eyes, i.e., egg-like. MUZZLE : Should show great strength and, though tapering, should not be " snipey." UNDER-JAW : Deep and strong. LIPS : Tight and clean. TEETH : Sound, strong, clean, and perfectly regular. An undershot or overhung mouth is objectionable. EARS : Small and thin, situated on the top of the skull fairly close together. Erect or semi-erect. EYES : Well sunken. As nearly black as possible, with a piercing glint, giving a keen expression. Small almond-shaped or triangular. Nearer the ears than nose, set closely together, and obliquely placed. NOSE : Black, with large developed nostrils. Bent downwards at the tip.

The NECK : Moderately long, tapering from shoulders to head. Very muscular, arched, and free from all traces of dewlap or throatiness. The SHOULDERS : Strong and muscular, but without any heaviness or loading. Shoulder-blades wide, flat and sloping, well back. No slackness or dip at the withers.

The CHEST : Broad, viewed from the front ; deep from withers to brisket.

The BODY : Ribs well sprung, i.e., rounded ; back ribs deep. Intercostal muscles well developed. The back short, strong and muscular. No drop at withers. Only slightly arched at loin. The TAIL : Short, fine, set on low, and carried horizontally ; thick where it joins the body, and tapering to a fine point.

The LEGS should be big-boned, but not coarse. FORELEGS : Moderately high, perfectly straight, and the dog must stand well on them. The elbows should not turn outwards. Pasterns strong and upright. HIND LEGS : Straight viewed from behind. Thighs very muscular. Hocks well let down, and the bone to the heels short and strong. The FEET : Round and compact, and the toes well arched ; resembling those of a cat, not a hare.

The COAT : Short, flat, rather harsh to the touch, and with a fine gloss. The skin should fit the dog tightly. The COLOUR : (For White) Pure white coat. (For Coloured and Stafford-shire) Colour (preferably brindle) to predominate.

FAULTS

Light bone. Legginess. Soft expression. Badly placed eyes. Light eyes. Domed skull. Butterfly nose. Pronounced cheekiness. Dish-faced. Lippiness. Throatiness. Teeth not meeting evenly. Long and slack back, Long, thick, and gay tail. Loose shoulders. Loaded shoulders. Crooked elbows. Weak pasterns. Cow hocks. Big and splay feet. Toes turning either in or out. Soft coat. Long coat. Narrow chest. Flat sides. Ewe neck. Markings on head and ticked coat, rose or button ears.

DISQUALIFICATIONS

Deafness. Wall eye. Wholly flesh coloured nose. Markings behind the set-on of head.

STANDARD OF POINTS

Neck, Shoulders, Body and Tail	..	..	..	..	20
Legs, and Feet	..	..	..	..	20
Head, Skull, Jaws, Lips, Teeth	..	..	..	..	20
Eyes and Expression ..	..	..	..	..	15
Movement	..	..	..	..	10
Condition and Pure White Body	..	..	..	..	10
Ears	..	..	..	..	5
					100

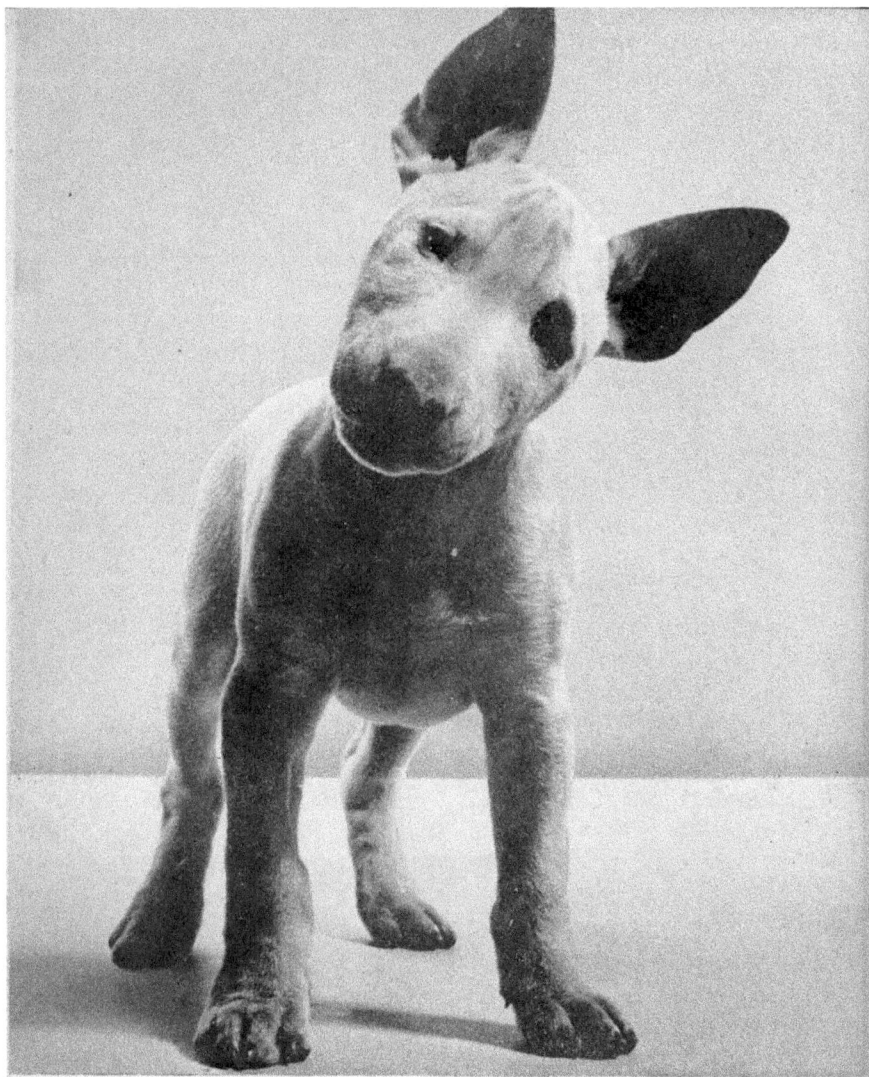

CAPTAIN HOOK, THE SON OF *Ch.* ROMANY RATHER LIGHTLY AND
Ch. RICKMAY ANBADAAD, AT 2 MONTHS.

THE LATE LT.-COL. V. WILBERFORCE WITH E.A. *Ch.* LIMPSFIELD CUTTY SARK AND COMMANDER.

Ch. COOLYN WONDER SON O'WHIRL-WIND.

(BRED AND OWNED IN U.S.A. BY COL. JAMES MARR.)

HARDY DES QUENIERES

(OWNED IN FRANCE BY DAPHNE HAMMOND.)

192

Ch. MADAME POMPADOUR OF
ERNICOR.

(OWNED AND BRED IN U.S.A.
BY ERNEST EBERHARD.)

Ch. HEIR APPARENT TO
MONTY-AYR.

($8\frac{1}{2}$ YEARS—U.S.A)

Int. Ch. RAYDIUM BRIGADIER
OF COOLYN HILL.

(BRED IN ENGLAND, FORMERLY
OWNED IN U.S.A. BY COL.
JAMES MARR.)

Ch. ORMANDY'S DANCING TIME.

(OWNED AND BRED BY RAYMOND OPPENHEIMER.)

THIS WONDERFUL BITCH PASSED AWAY. ONE OF THE BEST EVER PRODUCED.

Ch. ROMANY RELIANCE.

(OWNED BY MR. C. E. JENNINGS.)

Ch. ABRAXAS AUSTIN.

(OWNED AND BRED BY MISS DRUMMOND DICK.)

MRS. P. M. ADLAM WITH *Ch.* ROMA AND HER TWIN DAUGHTERS, *Ch.* BRENDON BARBED WIRE AND *Ch.* BRENDON BERYL.

MISS EVA WEATHERALL WITH ONE OF THE FAMOUS ORMANDYS.

Lightning Source UK Ltd.
Milton Keynes UK
UKHW04f1907130918
328855UK00001B/46/P

9 781445 528090